. . . .

What the People Know

The Joanna Jackson Goldman Memorial Lecture
on American Civilization and Government

. . . .

What the People Know

FREEDOM AND THE PRESS

. . . .

RICHARD REEVES

HARVARD UNIVERSITY PRESS

Cambridge, Massachusetts

London, England

1998

Library of Congress Cataloging-in-Publication Data

Reeves, Richard.
What the people know: freedom and the press /
Richard Reeves.
p. cm.
— (The Joanna Jackson Goldman memorial lecture
on American civilization and government)
Includes bibliographical references and index.
ISBN 0-674-61622-7 (alk. paper)
1. Reporters and reporting. 2. Journalism—Data processing.
I. Title. II. Series.
PN4781.R375 1998
070.1′72—dc21   98-22572

Designed by Gwen Nefsky Frankfeldt

This book is for Dick Harpster, Danny Blum,
Abe Rosenthal and Artie Gelb, Clay Felker,
Alice Mayhew, and Mr. Shawn,
the distinguished faculty
of my journalism
school.

Contents

Introduction   1

1 Covering the Naked Emperor   7

2 Technology Happens   29

3 If You Can't Beat 'Em, Buy 'Em   47

4 "The Tribe"   67

5 "Give Them What They Want!"   87

6 News as Entertainment   101

7 What's the Story?   113

Notes   133
Acknowledgments   141
Index   143

. . . .

What the People Know

Introduction

In the late 1960s, when John Lindsay was the mayor of New York, I was the City Hall bureau chief of the *New York Times*. One day, like most days, we were knocking His Honor around at a press conference, taking apart his numbers and just about everything else he had said in his efforts to defend one policy or another. "What do you think he's thinking when this is going on?" I asked another *Times*man, Maurice C. Carroll to his readers, "Mickey" to his friends. "What he always thinks," said Mickey. "'If you guys are so goddamn smart, how come you're not stockbrokers?'"

Mickey, it happened, had gotten me to New York. He lived in New Jersey and had seen a couple of stories of mine in the *Newark Evening News*. He was with the *New York Herald Tribune* in those days, when *Trib* writers like Tom Wolfe and Jimmy Breslin were heroes to young reporters like me. One night at a party, he'd come up to me and said, "How would you like to come to the *Trib*?" I'd answered that I would swim the Hudson every morning and work for free.

I was scared, of course, and with good reason. Only two

· 1 ·

years before that, I had been working for the *Phillipsburg Free Press,* a weekly paper I had started with another guy in Phillipsburg, New Jersey, where I was an engineer for a company called Ingersoll-Rand. I'd gone from the *Free Press* to the *Newark Evening News,* the state's biggest paper, because I'd realized that I hated being the boss. I just wanted to be a reporter.

I had stumbled upon an important fact: you become a reporter by saying you're a reporter. No qualifications. No license. Almost no training. "I became a newspaperman . . . I couldn't find honest employment"—that, famously, from Mark Twain. The employment I found at the end of 1963 was sitting up all night listening to the police radios of a couple of dozen towns in North Jersey. Sixty dollars a week. Thirty dollars in expenses if you used your own car. Ten dollars for each photo they used, fifteen if it was used on page one.

The *News* loved animal pictures. Dogs, lost and found. Kids and bunnies. Pet raccoons. Anything like that was usually fifteen dollars in the bank. One night, I hear a report from Succasunna—that's a town. An old lady's cat is up a tree. I'm on the phone to the cops before you can say "static."

"Hey, Sarge! Dick Reeves. *Newark News.* What are you going to do about the cat?"

"Nothing!" he says.

"What?" said I.

"Kid," he says. "You ever look up when you walk?"

"Yeah."

"Ever see any cat skeletons hanging from trees?"

Take that, Internet! Those were the days, my friend. We thought they'd never end. But they did. Talking about them

is Old Fartism, to borrow the phrase of Jon Katz, a newspaperman who leaped to the "new media" and then wrote
this: "Unable to embrace change or face the future, they have
opted instead to romanticize the past."[1]

The future began, I guess, with television and suburbs,
along with better roads and shopping centers, creating new
American lifestyles. Those changes killed a lot of newspapers, particularly "evening" papers. But, if truth be told,
for more than thirty years television news was part of the
good old days, at least in the news business, because the
people running TV news had been trained in print. More
often than not, the network news was paper news decorated
with moving pictures and talking heads. Soon reporters covering City Hall were paid more and dressed better, because
we got on the screen ourselves now and then.

But that's ending, too. Pictures meant more than words to
the next generation of television makers and their audience.
The new guys parodied their elders. Their work looked like
news, but after a while you realized it was actually a new mix
of entertainment elements—celebrities, blood, fire, sports,
sex, mixed with stories to make you feel good about yourself
and bad about your government. The American press is
tougher on government than on business for obvious reasons
that should be regularly repeated: corporations own newspapers and television stations, government does not; corporations sue newspapers and television stations, government
does not. And, or so, reporters know a lot more about government than they do about business.

We made more money and some of us became famous, but
the changes of the late twentieth century were not kind to

the carriers of the old torches of journalism. Our business, our craft, is in a crisis of change and redefinition. Was it only twenty years ago that for most Americans "the Press" meant network television news and their local newspaper? Now there are new words—"media," "communications"—floating in a confusion of realms: local and national newspapers; the tabloid titillators of both press and television; local television news linked by satellite to global sources; talk shows and more talk shows; web sites; prime-time news as entertainment; even things called "infomercials."

The dictionary, as always, is revealing. Webster's definition of "journalism" begins: "The occupation of reporting, writing, editing." (Webster's unabridged 1996 edition contains something like a personal attack on strivers like me. Its sample sentence for the word is: "He calls himself a historian, but his books are mere journalism.")

The definition of "communication" begins: "The act or process of communicating; the fact of being communicated."

I prefer A. J. Liebling's definition. The great *New Yorker* critic wrote:

> Communication means simply getting any idea across and has no intrinsic relation to the truth. It is neutral. It can be a peddler's tool or the weapon of a political knave, or the medium of a new religion.
> Q: What do you do for a living?
> A: I am a communicator.
> Q: What do you communicate? Scarlet fever? Apprehension?[2]

In a value-added world, journalists are still out there selling "values"—our own, of course. They are almost as simple as in this description by sociologist Herbert Gans: "The two that matter most in the newsroom are getting the story and getting it better and faster than their prime competitors—both among their colleagues and at rival news media. Personal political beliefs are left at home."[3]

All of this sounds more tribal than professional, and it is. When I use the words "press" and "reporters," I am describing my tribe, the nomads who hunt for truth, or at least facts, and gather branches and twigs to create some firelight.

Who needs this? A couple of years ago J. Randolph Murray, editor of the *Anniston Star* in Alabama, asked the question of the day at one of the many conferences journalists schedule to remind one another that they are alive, if not growing much anymore:

> Editors have been given the authority to make sense out of all this information by publishers, who can do that because they own the means to manufacture the product that distributes the information. When customers can take ownership of this information by sitting down at a keyboard, will they give the same authority to editors? And is there any evidence out there to indicate that the public will give or accept the authority editors now have? Why should they? Is it just a conceit of editors that we will do this because we have done it in the past?[4]

Eli Noam, a professor of economics at Columbia University, has a sensible answer to those questions. He has written on the future of book publishing and the romantic attachment of men and women to books, using an analogy that seems to apply to the old press as well: "Consider 'bread,' another word loaded with positive connotation. Consumption of bread has declined, and its centrality as a food item is nowhere near what it used to be."[5]

Well, we journalists have always been a crusty bunch. We certainly were when I made it to John Lindsay's City Hall. The culture gap between us and them showed at Christmas. The mayor, a man of patrician manner and Yale degrees, followed the tradition of giving each reporter a bottle. But instead of being filled with the usual Scotch whiskey, these bottles contained red wine, a beverage many regulars in the press room thought was served only in church. Today the papers have wine critics, and reporters are not quite sure where they fit in anymore.

Covering the Naked Emperor

Journalism has become too important to be left to journalists. We went too far, and technology has come too far, and now we are in trouble, much of it of our own making. "We," the press, are a likable bunch, working for newspapers and magazines, radio and television, and now "new media." We hate that last word. We are central to a critical paradox of our times. "The media" grow and multiply in leaps of bounding technologies, while journalism becomes more essential to life, liberty, and the pursuit of happiness. But at the same time, journalism is becoming a smaller and smaller part of something bigger and bigger: the delivery of all kinds of information and entertainment to paying customers.

Individual reporters, editors, and correspondents have more access and more influence, but to the movers and shakers of spreading information technologies, old and new, one manipulable digital picture may be worth a thousand ladies and gentlemen of the press.

And, strictly as business, a thousand reporters may be a pain in the assets. To our patrons, the lords of profit centers and purveyors of commingled fact, fact-based fiction, and semi-nonfiction, we may dwell someplace within a shrinking triangle of adolescence, obsolescence, and irrelevance. We, the press, may be going the way of blacksmiths. Same job: pounding hot stuff into useful but old-fashioned forms, like horseshoes. Or we could end up as bank tellers pushed aside for automatic teller machines—ATM journalism with slots to deposit or withdraw news.

Those are sad endings for men and women who see their labor as God's work. The cynicism that others see in us, we see as prolonged innocence (or adolescence) and idealism. It's fun being the one shouting that the emperor has no clothes. That is also the shout of real power, the old Fourth Estate role noted in London in 1828 by Lord Macaulay: "The gallery in which the reporters sit has become a fourth estate of the realm."[1] He put the quill-pen boys right up there with king, clergy, and Commons. It was a nice historical promotion. In revolutionary France, thirty years before, the Fourth Estate had been the mob shouting outside the palace in the filth of the streets.

In political terms, we did become the institutionalized mob. Sensationalism begins with the guy who shouts, "Look! Look at the emperor!" The bareness of public leaders was just one more fact we believed the public had a right to know. We are legends in our own minds, seekers of daily truth, watching the emperor and all others cloaked with power—excepting only ourselves from scalding scrutiny. Our power is exercised in the name and benefit of citizens busy with their own affairs—or so we like to think. I am partial to the self-description used by the *Express,* the weekly paper in the little Long Island town where my family has lived off-and-on for twenty years: "Reporting on Sag Harbor's births, deaths, politics and scandals, every week for the past 139 years."

But horseshoes and headlines may not make it against digital data. One of the country's most important newspapermen, Ron Martin, editor of the *Atlanta Journal-Constitution,* says the days when reporters went out and gathered stories and "wrote them up" are gone forever. Maybe he's right. What are we selling? What value are we adding? The official answer, quoted here from William Keller, managing editor of the *New York Times,* is: "We apply judgment to information."[2] Nice. But we may be talking to ourselves here. Maybe journalism is no more than the mission or the calling or a lifestyle celebrated by romantics like me. Perhaps it is just another endangered job description—the shared experience of a tribe who created their own traditions and values, and had a hell of a good time doing it. Maybe it's just habits and tricks passed from hand to hand, or mouth to mouth.

The questions are painful for all of us who believe in what we do. There seems to be a real chance that what we have learned and practiced could get lost in the chase and race of this end-of-the-century round of spectacular and profitable technological shuffling.

Like the automobiles and mass production that doomed smithing at the end of the nineteenth century, the exploding new technologies of our times should prove to be a boon to humankind. But the initial exploitation of the technology has been creating new words and meanings, many hidden in dehumanizing little digits and definitions. "Media," above all, with its many refinements and manifestations; and then "the product," "data," "content," "platform," "niche," "brand," "server," "market research," "profit center."

We prefer older words and legends. Though it was published before my time, I have always been charmed by a defining passage written in 1932 by Stanley Walker, the city editor of the *New York Herald Tribune:*

> What makes a good newspaperman? The answer is easy. He knows everything. He is aware not only of what goes on in the world today, but his brain is a repository of the accumulated wisdom of the ages . . . He is not only handsome, but he has the physical strength which enables him to perform great feats of energy. He can go for nights on end without sleep. He dresses well and talks with charm. Men admire him; women adore him; tycoons and statesmen are willing to share their secrets with him . . . He hates lies and meanness and sham, but keeps his temper. He is loyal to his paper and to what he looks upon as his profession; whether it is a profession, or merely a craft, he resents efforts to debase it. When he dies, a lot of people are sorry, and some of them remember him for several days.[3]

Thus the troops define themselves. But the officers of the commanding new technologies and distant corporate generals saw this all quite differently. With the wind at their backs as economics triumphed over politics in American life during the 1980s and 1990s, journalism was invaded and occupied; some would say rationalized or put in its place. At the same time, professors of journalism and other academics were taking our name and whatever heritage we had and turning schools of journalism into schools of "communications"—a tabula rasa that meant whatever served their purposes. Inside newsrooms, our old forts, we underrated the attacks and overrated ourselves. We were at our self-congratulatory worst in the heady hearing rooms and dining rooms of Washington, where the rough charm of the old tribe was beginning to transform itself into the mumbling chants of a priesthood. Then we overreached, misjudging the mission and our own capabilities.

The misjudgments did not begin with the temporary victory of journalists over politicians in the political battle called Watergate, but that struggle was probably the signal event in the rise of self-destructive journalistic hubris in the 1970s and beyond. There was a power vacuum at the top in the United States of the 1960s and 1970s—a slide accelerated by a bad war and good new technologies and by the decadence of shared power worship in the capital city. The slippery slope of capital power was lubricated by wandering streams of perceived public opinion, gauged almost hourly by new polls, by surveys and focus groups. Looking at the numbers, most any numbers, politicians and elected officials were less and less inclined to risk using the power given them by the voters of the republic. Politicians understood that their business, getting elected, was not about making friends but about avoiding organized enemies. If polls showed they were going to get into trouble by being decisive, they decided not to decide.

War, race, and the unclothing of Richard Nixon checked political leadership. An unpopular war in Vietnam, a reluctance to get involved in racial disputes like the integration of public schools, and then the disgrace of the thirty-seventh president drew the courts and the press into using or trying to use power they had never had before. Judges took over school districts and schoolbusing, prisons and hospitals. Reporters took on priestly duties of the political establishment, stepping up to the bully pulpit of moral leadership. We thought the public, the American people, deserved better than what they had. Self-righteously, we thought *we* deserved more, too—and that maybe we had more to offer the people than just watching and reporting on the official institutions of the democracy.

At the beginning of the twentieth century, Joseph Pulitzer, the publisher and founder of the first journalism school in the country (at Columbia University, after Harvard dismissed the idea), was asked to define the word "journalism" and said: "A journalist is the lookout on the bridge of the ship of state."[4] Would that it were true. If it ever was, there came a time when the lookout wondered whether he knew more about where the ship of state should go than did the captain and the rest of the crew. In 1975 the general manager of the Associated Press, Wes Gallagher, invoked the Constitution in declaring that the press was ready and willing to save the nation from itself: "The First Amendment is more than just a hunting license. We must put before the public ways and means of strengthening the institutions that protect us all—not tear them down."[5]

That declaration could be seen as a symbolic peak of the rising of the press which began in the late 1950s, with the introduction of a new newsbox, television, into most American homes. There were new stories, too, dramatic and photogenic stories: the civil rights marches of black Americans and blood and guts in Vietnam. On the first, government was divided and thus weakened, North versus South again, federal power versus "states' rights." On Vietnam, the government was ineffective, if not misguided. The press did not initiate the struggle for civil rights, or the undeclared Asian war, or the antiwar movement at home. In fact, we showed up a bit late—as we did on the other big stories of my lifetime: feminism, environmentalism, religious revival, conservative antigovernment populism, and the ascendance of economics over politics.

Those dramatic stories, promoted on television, attracted some of the best and brightest of young Americans into the news business. Highly educated men and women who wanted to make a difference—and make it fast!—saw journalism as a way to do just that, without the tedious apprenticeships of government, law, and old-fashioned commerce. With notebooks and cameras, young warriors of the word *were* making a difference. The best example was David Halberstam, Harvard '57, who went to Mississippi at twenty-two and Vietnam at twenty-seven. Television was also turning young correspondents into stars. A decade later, particularly in Washington, Watergate turned them into heroes, beginning with Bob Woodward and Carl Bernstein of the *Washington Post*.

Journalism, in fact, was becoming better than it had ever been. The pay was getting better, too. But the attraction of journalism, the excitement, was what it had always been, being wherever the action was. Being young and smart and powerful was a bonus.

Carelessly and systematically, the high-riding Washington press corps and provincial imitators diminished politicians and governors, subjecting them to public scorn. Our message was simple: "They're all bums. Don't believe them! Don't listen to them!'" Chapter and verse: bums and liars! There was a telling moment, totally fictional, in Oliver Stone's 1995 film *Nixon*. The president, confronted by a war protester, tells her he is trying to end the war.

> *Young Woman:* You don't want the war. We don't want the war. The Vietnamese don't want the war. So why does it go on?
>
> [Nixon hesitates, out of answers.]
>
> *Young Woman:* Someone wants it . . . [A realization] You can't stop it, can you . . . Even if you wanted to. Because it's not you. It's the system. And the system won't let you stop it . . .
>
> [The girl transfixes him with her eyes . . .]

The shorthand in the news business has always been the same: There is only one way to look at politicians—down! But after Watergate, we went wilder: Throw them out, despise them, they're irrelevant. Don't read about them. Ignore their self-serving yatter on television. I. F. Stone, a reporter and pamphleteer of the Left, became a hero to many of the young reporters of the 1960s and 1970s, saying things like this: "Every government is run by liars, and nothing they say should be believed."[6]

Great stuff, and it worked! There was more than a little irony in this, though. We, after all, always functioned as stenographers to the powers-that-were, the naked emperors and assorted other bums. So even as we took down their words, we took down politicians and politics, without pausing to think that maybe we would go down with them, like mating eagles falling from the sky with their claws locked together. Or—to switch birds—we killed the golden goose. Why should solid folk watch and read about bums and liars? "What do you think you're doing?" said a politician who noticed, Barney Frank, a congressman from Massachusetts. "You people celebrate failure and ignore success. Nothing about government is done as incompetently as the reporting of it."[7]

That is an overstatement. But the credibility of the press is a fair target. If we are in decline, it is because we have again fallen into the trap of ignoring what government does and focusing on what it has done wrong. Mistakes were made, as politicians say in excusing themselves. One of the press's mistakes, as recorded by Shirley Biagi, a journalism professor at California State University, was crossing this line: "The press in America, it is generally agreed, don't tell you what to think but do tell you what and whom to think about."[8]

We carried ourselves away—and not for the first time. It was in 1906 that Theodore Roosevelt pinned the name "muckrakers" on investigative magazine editors and writers, taking the word from *The Pilgrim's Progress* (1678), by John Bunyan—it's his term for men who look nowhere but down. The press of the early twentieth century seized the name as a badge of honor. We still wear it as tribute to the terrific and necessary work done by Lincoln Steffens, Ida Tarbell, Will Irwin, and other reporters at a time when magazines were the only national mass medium. But Roosevelt did not mean it as a compliment, and his words, spoken almost a century ago, resonate as a warning: "The men with the muckrakes are often indispensable to the well-being of society, but only if they know when to stop raking the muck, and to look upward to the celestial crown above them. If they gradually grow to feel that the whole world is nothing but muck, their power of usefulness is gone."

The history of journalism is a history of surges, of stepping in and up when other institutions were slow to change in times of political crisis or technological change—but then going too far or stumbling into pits of trivia, losing the trust of the public or the tolerance of powerful allies, Teddy Roosevelt in this case. Too late, we would remember or be reminded that the accepted and acceptable role of a robust press, our maximum claim, is a promise and social contract to keep an eye on politics and government for readers and viewers busy in the pursuit of happiness. The claim, which has to be regularly renewed—What have you done for me lately?—is based on a few words in the United States Constitution. The First Amendment: "Congress shall make no law respecting an establishment of religion, or prohibiting the free exercise thereof; or abridging the freedom of speech, or of the press . . ."

Whatever those words meant in 1789, when the press disseminated opinion (the gathering of "news" was yet to be invented), the business of journalism used them to build a great fortress. By the 1960s the press had persuaded both public and power to accept our privileged definition of those words. That effort may have peaked in the 1970s, when a Supreme Court Justice, Potter Stewart, wrote:

"The primary purpose of the constitutional guarantee of a free press was . . . to create a fourth institution outside the government as an additional check on the three official branches . . . The relevant metaphor is of the Fourth Estate

. . . The Free Press Clause extends protection to an institution."

So Oscar Wilde, who disliked both America and the press, could say: "In America, the president reigns for four years and journalism governs for ever and ever."[9]

That was the Fourth Estate's role and responsibility, accepted (extraconstitutionally) by the citizens of the democracy. But covering public officials and their works mattered less and less once our audience turned away from the rulers we told them were not worth watching. But then, the press didn't matter much either, did it? Why watch the nightly news on television? Why buy a paper every day, unless you were looking for a job or wanted to check the prices at the supermarket?

Politicians, of course, were doing their bit toward self-destruction. Dense beyond belief, the seekers of citizens' votes concentrated their own efforts on raising money to produce television commercials telling voters that their opponents were even worse than they were. Half of those candidates won—but which half didn't much matter, since the paid political advertising, along with negative press, was effectively convincing most citizens that all politicians were screwing most of the public most of time.

Press and politicians were coming to hate each other. A politically gifted young president, who won election by getting around political reporters preaching modern puritanism, thought he could as easily get around the overblown White House press corps. On March 20, 1993, President Bill Clinton spoke at the annual dinner of the White House Radio and Television Correspondents Association and said: "You know why I can stiff you on press conferences? Because Larry King liberated me from you by giving me the American people directly."

Apparently no one had told him that the American people did not want their president in their homes full time, or that Larry King and Oprah Winfrey and Arsenio Hall did not cover White House briefings and congressional hearings. One can argue about how well or even how much the priests of the capital gang cover governance, but they are the only people who do it systematically every day. The reporters at the White House and on Capitol Hill specialize in institutional memory, a routine of cataloguing and checking facts that has been greatly enhanced by the speed and unforgiving memory of computers. In a traditional leaving-the-beat thumbsucker that I. F. Stone would have applauded, Ruth Marcus, the White House correspondent for the *Washington Post,* wrote of her nineteen months covering Clinton under the three-column headline, "The White House Isn't Telling Us the Truth."[10]

You did not need Diogenes at your side to realize that some of the president's problems with the press, an unpleasant gamut from Serbia to sex, were actually his own problems with the truth, the whole truth, and nothing but the truth. "Which one do you want?"—that's the punch line of an old courthouse joke.

But there is more to being president than pleasing reporters. Clinton avoided the press for weeks at a time, ignoring as much as he could the urgings of his staff to get out there and explain himself. Clinton told his assistants that all the reporters would do was try to trip him up with scandal questions on women and Whitewater (a sticky Arkansas real estate deal in which the Clintons had invested while he was governor). He was exactly right about that.

One of the few conferences he agreed to do took place on the evening of March 24, 1994.

"With the Congress beginning its Easter recess tomorrow, this is a good time to assess the real work we are getting done," he began. In his opening statement, he touched on the day's events—the assassination of the leading candidate for the presidency of Mexico, an Air Force transport crash, statistics showing an increase of two million jobs in the United States, the progress of health care and welfare reform legislation, fighting between Serbs and Muslims in Bosnia, nuclear weapons in North Korea, human rights in China, and the return of American troops from Somalia. He reviewed the progress of health care and welfare reform bills, a crime bill, and campaign reform legislation being debated in Congress. "America's efforts have helped to bring much needed calm to Sarajevo and led to an important political accord between the Bosnian Muslims and Croats," he said. "We'll continue our efforts to stop North Korea's nuclear program and to seek progress on human rights in China . . . This Friday, a week ahead of schedule, our troops will return home from So-malia."

"Terry?" he said, asking for the first question from the reporters in front of him. There were twenty-one questions: one on health care, another on American efforts to block the development of nuclear weapons in North Korea, another on the assassination of Mexico's presidential candidate—and eighteen on Whitewater and Clinton's family finances.

He felt victimized. "Let me tell you what my wife and I spent the Eighties doing. I was the lowest-paid governor of any state in the country. I don't complain about it. I was proud of that. I didn't do it for the money. I worked on creating jobs and improving education for the children of my state. My wife worked in a law firm . . . She never took any money for any work she did for the state . . . Every year she gave an enormous percentage of her time to public service work, helping children and helping education."

Five months after that, I happened to be in the White House talking with the president's national security adviser, Anthony Lake. He was in despair over that day's lead story in the *New York Times*. "TOP U.S. OFFICIALS DIVIDED IN DEBATE ON INVADING HAITI," read the headline. The reporter, Elaine Sciolino, wrote:

> This division became evident, officials said, at a meeting of Clinton's top national security advisers on Tuesday at the White House. The meeting had been called to draw up recommendations for the President.
> Defense Secretary William J. Perry opposed . . .
> But Deputy Secretary Strobe Talbott . . .
> In a sharp exchange, Mr. Perry countered that Mr. Talbott represented a strange morality. He argued that it would be immoral for the United States not to do whatever it could to avoid the loss of lives of American soldiers and the expenditure of taxpayers' money.[11]

The piece went on for thirty paragraphs, reporting arguments of and between "principals," as the highest officials call one another. There had been only eight people in the room on the ground floor of the White House, but the reporter from the *Times* got it practically word-for-word. One or more of the principals must have passed the recommendations on to the *Times* (and the world) before they were ever conveyed to the president.

"How? Why?" Lake said. "Who?"

"Who" is us. "How" is by offering government officials, usually dedicated mid-level types, the chance to put forward their agendas by leaking to and through us. "We" are the way "they" get their ideas out or neutralize other ideas or other rivals. "Why"? Because that is what we do—and from my perspective, we do too little of it rather than too much.

Leaks are central to American freedom. Tyranny depends on government secrecy. I didn't say that—Patrick Henry did. These were his words:

"The press must prevent officials from covering with the veil of secrecy the common routine of business, for the liberties of the people never were, or never will be, secure when the transactions of their rulers may be concealed from them."

That thought went global in 1994, when a million people were massacred in the African country of Rwanda—even though a United Nations military mission knew in advance of the killing plan. An inquiry concluded that the mission might have prevented the genocide by leaking to the *New York Times* rather than reporting to their superiors.[12]

So give me leaking or give me death. The United States does not have a tradition of resignation in protest, as Great Britain, for one, does. In London, through history, public officials high and low have quit over secret policy disputes within the government, going public with their gripes or alarms. We do it differently. Americans tend to hang in there, telling themselves they have more influence inside than out in the cold. The brave and principled ones leak the truth and let the public judge for itself who's right and who's wrong.

That is not to say Americans always prefer truth to loyalty. Historically, the opposite has often been true. The most famous American resignation in protest came in 1915, when Secretary of State William Jennings Bryan quit and went lecturing to charge that his boss, President Woodrow Wilson, was preparing to lead the country into World War I even as he was campaigning promising the opposite. Bryan, who long had been among the most popular of Americans, was jeered and taunted from coast to coast for telling the truth. Since then, less well-known whistle blowers—say, the military bureaucrats who speak truth to power about Defense Department cost overruns and faked test results—have paid a high price for their leaking heroism. More often than not, they have never worked again in their chosen fields.

Tony Lake knows the game as well as anyone. He resigned, quietly, from a staff position at the National Security Council in 1970 because he objected to secret American bombing in Southeast Asia. But he kept his silence. This is not to say that all resignations or all leaking is altruistic. Personal hatred or revenge is as common a motive for leaks as concerns over the state of the nation. But most leaks have important and legitimate public policy objectives. Trial balloons test public reaction to appointments or policy before a name or initiative is announced. Others, on the "Deep Throat" model, are villainy alerts. Many are attempts to get a viewpoint or objection to the president. If truth be told, presidents don't always read memos or listen carefully to subordinates, but they all read the papers—at least so far.

That said, presidents and their advisers generally get less and less rational about any and all leaks that do not originate with them. This is part of a May 1961 memo to President Kennedy from his national security adviser, McGeorge Bundy: "A couple of weeks ago, you asked me to begin to meet you [regularly in the morning]. I have succeeded in catching you on three mornings, for a total of about eight minutes. Moreover, six of the eight minutes were an exercise in who leaked [to the newspapers] and why."[13]

Presidents still can't stop leaks—that's what President Nixon's villainous "plumbers" were about—but this is the whole idea. In fact, presidents often function as leakers-in-chief, and secretaries of state are right up there, too. During the presidency of George Bush, a magazine writer named Michael Kelly was allowed to follow Secretary of State James Baker on his daily rounds and reported, quite seriously, that Baker spent thirty-five hours a week leaking to the press exactly what he wanted to be in the press.

Most government officials do not leak. But they all know why it is done and why it may be necessary. This is the testimony of a young naval officer named Brian Lamb, who was assigned to the public affairs office of the Department of Defense during the war in Vietnam. Thirty years after that, in 1997, when he was running C-Span, the public affairs television network he'd created, he was interviewed by Thomas Hazlett of *Reason* magazine. In his flat Indiana voice, he spoke about his Pentagon service:

I spent two years there answering questions for the networks
. . . It wasn't an important job, but for me it was a great window on the world. It was my first education into how news was made, and what motivated correspondents and what motivated the government, how government attempted to shade

and cover up and lie, and how the media in some cases would be a willing accomplice. [Defense Secretary] Robert McNamara used to have a weekly meeting with the press on Thursday afternoons. The media sat around his dining room table and asked him questions. Whenever they used the material, they could only quote "U.S. officials" . . . It allowed the government to get its message out and it allowed the media to have a story. Every Friday morning in the *New York Times* a lead story said, "U.S. officials predict the bombing of the North will end in two months." And those twenty-five reporters sitting around the table all knew who said it, but the public never did.

It seemed to me to be a fraud. I know the people involved in it then thought they were doing honorable work, and no one was per se lying at a particular meeting, although the Secretary didn't tell the truth all the time . . . I kept saying to myself, there's something wrong there. This ought to be an open situation, and the more closed it is and the more insular it is, the more both sides can fool the public for their own reasons. And we found ourselves in a major war, 500,000 troops deployed and 58,000 people killed.

Perhaps it would have been better if Lieutenant Lamb had become an anonymous source rather than Secretary McNamara. But really there is no such thing as an "anonymous source." As far as the public was concerned, the source in both 1964 and 1994 was not McNamara or one of Lake's colleagues; the source on both occasions was the *New York Times*. You either believe the *Times* or you don't. You either believe CBS News or the *National Enquirer* or you don't. A citizen judges news by the source. I have always been surprised by the relative immunity readers grant to newspapers and television stations. If you think we're making quotes up or distorting discussion and action, organize against us. What is the point of moaning about the anonymous "they" supposedly saying or doing these things? It's us! The press. We are the source, and we should be accountable for every single word. Bang on our windows. Picket our doors. Cancel subscriptions. Boycott our advertisers. Organize! If you don't believe us, make us tell you where we're getting this stuff.

No government is safe from leaks; no people are safe without them. But the same could be said of truth itself. The object of leaked truth can be noble or evil. More often than not, it is meant to be destructive in some way—gritty drippings into the gears of power.

Months after Sciolino's Haiti story in 1994, both the president and his vice-president, Albert Gore, were still talking about that particular frustration, telling me in separate conversations that they thought they were getting close to figuring out who had leaked to Sciolino. Lake detailed the internal reaction to such leaks: White House meetings were getting smaller and smaller, and less and less was put in writing. As a result, dialogue inside Clinton's White House was becoming more and more distorted. "You lose expertise, you lose precision," said Lake in an interview. "People are afraid to speak their minds, or they say things precisely because they want them to be in tomorrow's *Washington Post*."

Leaks are the wild cards of governance. What the people know and when they know it are the engine of democracy. Leaks change the timing.

On a greater scale, that is what technology has done—it has changed what the people know and when and how they find out. For almost two hundred years, presidents had effective control over the flow of information to the nation. Franklin D. Roosevelt was able to hide the real and devastating details of the destruction of the United States Navy at Pearl Harbor on December 7, 1941. Almost one hundred years earlier, President James Polk had been able to suppress the news of the discovery of gold in California, gaining time to send troops west to ensure American control of that suddenly rich and critical territory. Now presidents get the news at the same time the rest of us do, and often in the same way—often from the Cable News Network (CNN).

President Clinton's first shot in anger was a Tomahawk missile strike from U.S. warships in the Persian Gulf. The target was the headquarters of Iraq's intelligence agency in Baghdad—in retaliation, the president said, for a planned assassination of former president George Bush during a visit to Kuwait. Eager to announce the strike live on the nightly news, Clinton was frustrated because he could not get information on whether or not the missiles had hit their target. An aide, David Gergen, finally suggested calling CNN rather than the CIA. At 6:30 P.M., Tom Johnson, the president of Cable News Network, was able to tell the President of the United States that the Tomahawks had indeed hit their target. Then the commander-in-chief went live on CNN (and the three older networks) to announce the news to the people who had told him.

The new information technology can be incredibly democratizing. That was dramatized for me on a Monday morning in October 1993, when I appeared on NBC's *Today* show. Sitting in the studio, I watched the segment that preceded mine—an interview with three wives of American soldiers in Somalia. One of the wives was weeping, saying that their husbands were going to be killed and their children would be orphans. It was, the women said, all President Clinton's fault for sending their men to Africa on what was supposed to be a United Nations humanitarian mission to a country being decimated by famine and war. And now Somalis were shooting at Americans. Then, thanks to another miracle of modern technology, the husbands called in from Mogadishu on cellular phones, their words bouncing off satellites in the stratosphere, to say that their commander-in-chief had told them there was no danger. My first thought was that everyone is the same size on television. My second thought was that Lincoln and Roosevelt had been lucky that satellites and cellulars hadn't existed when the battle of Gettysburg was fought in 1863 or when Allied troops landed on the beaches of Normandy in 1944.

The electronic din can truly make all men equal. These days, the president, Rush Limbaugh, the *New York Times,* the *National Enquirer,* the CIA, the Pharmaceutical Manufacturers Association, Larry King, soldiers' wives, and you and I pretty much get the news at the same time: all information and all images are created equal. All "surveys," all faxes, all faces. If that's the way it is now, so much for old-time journalism. Thanks for the memory—see you all on the Internet or a cable channel with a triple-digit number.

Technology Happens

"There are going to be so many new voices in this world. How we practice our profession is going to be increasingly important," said John Haile, editor of the *Orlando Sentinel*, at the 1995 convention of the American Society of Newspaper Editors, during one of the panels about where journalism is going—if we are going anywhere. "The traditional entry barriers in our business are coming down really fast. Somebody with a computer and a good idea can get into business and compete with us overnight. Somebody can become a publisher without any training . . . We have to distinguish ourselves from those masses by being better at what we traditionally do."

"Forgive me for being blunt," began the next speaker, Andy Grove, the president of Intel, a computer chip company that channels millions of those new voices. "You seem to be somewhat oblivious. You think you are in the forefront of the revolution, but there are some seven million people who get at least a portion of their news through on-line services, not one of which was started by newspapers or associated with newspapers."

Technology happens. And the world is never the same again. The Pony Express, the West's fastest information delivery system, went out of business on October 26, 1861, two days after America was wired for the first time—by telegraph lines.[1] That was a bad day for blacksmiths.

Nothing as terminal has happened yet in the most recent cycle of wiring, unwiring, and unraveling. In fact, no one, least of all the players, is sure how this game will end, as innovation begets innovation. David Burke, a former president of CBS News and vice-president of ABC News, makes this educated guess: "Network news is dead. The networks offer news by appointment. The consumer has to meet us at a specific time, say 7 P.M. The new technologies will provide news on demand—what you want to know when you want it."[2]

This already seems to be true for perhaps 20 million Americans, the ones with a couple of thousand dollars of expendable income to buy a personal computer and accessories. For the moment, this has created another information (or empowerment) gap between rich and poor. We can only guess how long it will be before PCs are available for all, as commonplace as telephones, and whether the current Windows-based systems will prevail as other technologies come on line.

My own worries about the technology have less to do with how I get my news than with how it is gathered and prepared for transmission. I worry about the future of writing—if it has a future. I exaggerate, of course. But I do see troubling portents in Windows '95, Microsoft's pictographic and thus universal language, using icons and mice rather than letters and keystroking. What next? I would guess voice-controlled computers—in offices, homes, cars, pockets—that will accept and send audible directions and information.

The technology is already available for revolution. Waking up my computer one morning not long ago, I was greeted by an advertisement for a piece of software called Voice E-Mail, $29.95 if you "Click now!" It wanted me to talk to it. This is what it had to say:

"While most computer users type an average of 20–30 words per minute, and while most professional typists average 60–80 words per minute, human speech averages 200–250 words per minute . . . There is no need for editing, no need for spelling, no need for grammar or punctuation checking!"

So much for me—or for what I know how to do. I should be used to it by now. I graduated from college as a slide-rule, vacuum-tube engineer. Within a few years, Texas Instruments was selling most of what I knew for about ten dollars—in the form of a pocket calculator. But I had learned to write. You could always get work if you were good at editing, spelling, grammar, punctuation. Now they are going to sell my skills again.

Why write when you can talk? Most people think writing is torture, and they have no patience or time for reading. But those same folks love to talk and listen. Well, the hardware exists, and software is being developed to make it possible to function by directing streams-of-verbal-consciousness at refrigerators, televisions, stores, dashboards, school desks, and flush toilets. Such voice-recognition technology is being developed by Microsoft, IBM, and Lucent and will eventually be able to understand any and all languages.

Will that be the next big thing? Who knows? Creating the

software is labor-intensive, takes a lot of man-hours. So the capability of the programs lags behind that of the hardware—and government, you, and me lag behind all of it. Keeping up is difficult even for the men and women who spend all their time pushing the envelopes of technology. There's simply too much happening. So there is a great deal of ignorance in media land. A year after Andy Grove offered his critique of the old to the 1995 ASNE convention, Ted Leonsis, the forty-year-old president of the Internet server America Online, was a speaker at the organization's next annual conference in Washington. He began by adding a million to the number of people distancing themselves from traditional news servers. "This is a mass medium in development—eight million people are paying us twenty dollars a month," he said. "You're in crisis. If you lose 10 percent of classified [advertising], you go from profitable to unprofitable . . . In the future, editors will be bartenders—filling the individual orders of customers . . . We're oxygen. Get used to it!"

Then, sweeping a copy of the day's *New York Times* from under his chair, he riffled through the pages to make a point, and ended by pronouncing: "See? There is no local news in here. Get local!"

An editor in the audience called out a correction: "That's the National Edition of the *Times* you have. Local news has its own section in New York."

The greatest threat to the oldies—newspapers, magazines, radio and network television—is the generation gap. Grove, who was sixty-one, spoke for the old this time:

> I like the crinkling of paper. I like tearing things out much
> better than I like reading a screen. But I do like reading my

news the earliest I can . . . When you get into the situation where you can basically read tomorrow's news on a computer screen today, the value of tomorrow's newspaper is going to diminish some . . . The population that is young today relies on computers for work, learning, and play. These people have grown up with the computer screen. You are sitting on a demographic time bomb.

Months later, I thought I heard a little "boom!" in a conversation I was having with a successful Los Angeles restaurateur named Sean MacPherson, thirty-two years old and rich enough to wear lumberjack shirts and shoulder-length hair as he visits his properties.

"I see the restaurants in my head as three-dimensional artworks, and I get great satisfaction if I can make that happen, bring them to life. I'm applying style. I think Marshall McLuhan was right about the medium being the message."

"You've read McLuhan?" I asked.

"No. No, I know it from that Woody Allen movie."

He saw disappointment or something pass over my face. Then he said: "No one reads, you know. They speak television, and it's just fine!"

I read. I reread Marshall McLuhan while thinking about all this. This is the way Lewis Lapham, the editor of *Harper's* magazine, saw it in his introduction to MIT Press's 1994 edition of McLuhan's *Understanding Media*:

> The world that McLuhan describes has taken shape during my own lifetime, and within the span of my own experience. I can remember that as recently as 1960 it was still possible to make distinctions between the several forms of what were then known as the lively arts. The audiences recognized the differences between journalism, literature, politics, and the

movies . . . but then the lines between fact and fiction blurred, became as irrelevant as they were difficult to distinguish, the lively arts fused into the amalgam of forms known as the media. News was entertainment and entertainment was news.

And what of the "old" news? "Pooped, confused and broke," wrote Jon Katz, a former editor of the *Dallas Times Herald* who left what he called the Old Fartism of newspapers to go to the Internet. This is his description of the "new news": "Dazzling, adolescent, irresponsible, fearless, frightening and powerful . . . A heady concoction, part Hollywood film and TV movie, part pop music and pop art, mixed with popular culture and celebrity magazines, tabloid telecasts, cable and home video."[3]

"Concoction" is the key word here: technological developments are continually changing the mix. One glimpse of the future introduced early in 1997 was the "Live Video Insertion System," or LVIS (Get it? "Elvis"), which can digitally create logos or ads on stadium walls or even on playing fields. "The virtual billboard" can make viewers think there is a giant "Coke" symbol at midfield during a Super Bowl. Television viewers see the big sign; old-timers actually in the stadium see nothing but grass.

By the end of 1997, individuals could buy the future and manipulate the past—or so they were told in a two-page Christmas advertisement placed in dozens of magazines by Hewlett-Packard. The product being pushed was the "HP Smart System." The system included a digital camera and a printer, which with Microsoft's "PictureIt!" software "can adjust exposures, change colors, crop and manipulate images—

all as creativity dictates." The ad promises "the first pictures of the future."

And it delivers. The first of the pages offers old-fashioned Kodak-like reality, a family photo in front of a Christmas tree. Mom, dad, and daughter Megan are dressed all in Gap, but son Patrick is in leather, accented by boots, topped off by a flaming-red spiked Mohawk. On the second page, the photo has become a new-fashioned card. Under "Season's Greetings, Grandma!" everything is the same except for Patrick, now in a pullover and chinos, his hair brown and short. The headline is "Grandmother spared holiday shock, heirs breathe easily."

What happened? Technology happened, says the copy: "Photo of the Clifford Family, after scanning in and manipulating earlier photo of Patrick from pre-collegiate period— sparing Grandmother a shock, which might have led to possible designation of new heirs."

When I visited Hewlett-Packard's website, I was told by Vyomesh Joshi, general manager of the company's Home Imaging Division, that this is all about shoeboxes full of memorabilia somewhere in the back of a closet. "Take shoebox collections of slides, prints, and negatives from the last one hundred years," he said, "and enhance them for insertion into collages, family histories, and posters."

He was right. It was amazing. I could move people, trees, anything from one photo to another. The best ones in my family were not in shoeboxes, though. Because of our peculiar family history, we kept them in safe-deposit boxes in a Swiss bank. I had great fun with them. You know the picture of Saddam Hussein and me dancing in that basement disco? I made him into Madeleine Albright. The one of Grandpa shaking hands with Hitler? I changed Hitler to Roosevelt. I made that all up. The last paragraph, I mean. The advertisement and the technical stuff are all as real as negatives used to be. Remember those movie scenes where the good guy says, "Don't try to fool me, Boris—I want the negatives, too." The same was true in real life. People with uniforms or clubs and guns could smash news cameras and ruin the film. But forget all that. With digital cameras, there are no negatives—images can be sent electronically and instantaneously to the CIA, NBC, the *New York Times,* or the *National Enquirer* for manipulation "as creativity dictates."

Technology happens fast. When Ronald Reagan was elected president in 1980, there was no PhotoSmart—and no CNN, VCR, CD, PC, or fax. Going back twenty more years to the election of President John F. Kennedy in 1960, communications depended on such artifacts as flashbulbs, mimeographs, and carbon paper. The times, *Times,* and machines change. The next changes could hit folks like me where it hurts, right in the old occupation. If the word goes audible, as I think it will, a lot of people, younger ones, may dictate better than I can write.

Technology doesn't care about such things. It is and always has been a perfect fit with news, because speed is all in delivering information when and where it is useful. So our story is told in terms of both humans and laws and of mechanics and machinery. For centuries, information was a product that could move no faster than a horse or a sailing ship. For four hundred of those years, the technology of printing relied more or less on the flatbed screw press that

Johannes Gutenberg devised in 1455 for printing Bibles. The pace of the world was such that in 1819, when local dignitaries were invited to a test ride on the first railroad line in the United States (a few miles of what became the Baltimore and Ohio), they were asked to take notes along the way—because many scientists believed that the human mind would not be able to function at the unheard-of speed of eighteen miles per hour.[4]

The great breakthrough in modern mass communication was the telegraph. What we call journalism was built on dits and dahs tapping along copper wire strung high on poles from the Atlantic to the Pacific. It was the technology of the telegraph that produced the wire services and the "Who . . . What . . . Where . . . When" leads, to make sure that as much "news" as possible would be transmitted up front just in case a wire broke or was attacked by Indians, weather, or sparrows.

If there was a single man, genius unleashed, who invented what we call news, it was James Gordon Bennett, who devised systems and schemes to define and gather "news" as the founder, in 1835, of the *New York Herald*. Until he came on the scene, American newspapering was still an extension of the British editorial press, more opinion than fact, more true than not, correspondence rather than reporting, all done for small numbers of the better classes. This was Bennett in New York, as described by Will Irwin, a former newspaper reporter and editor of *McClure's* magazine, who was commissioned by *Collier's* magazine to write a history and analysis of the American press that was published serially over fifteen weeks in 1911:

Bennett, ruthless, short in the conscience, expressing in his own person all the atrocious bad taste of his age, was yet a genius . . . Through two stormy, dirty decades he set an idea of news that we have proceeded on ever since. "I renounce all so-called principles," he said in his salutary. He set out to find news and to print it first . . . Working with the tools he had, Bennett performed prodigies. His marine couriers transmitted European news hours ahead of his rivals; he kept in touch with our borders by private lines of pony messengers. Before the telegraph he had experimented with schemes for quicker transmission by semaphore, pneumatic tube and even balloon; the poles on the first telegraph lines were still green when Bennett had made the invention part of his own system . . . In getting news he was equally keen and eager. He, first of all Americans, violated the sanctity of the home. He invaded Wall Street. Day by day he revealed the financial situation exactly as it seemed to him—for he was long his own Wall Street reporter . . . He found a method of watching systematically the police stations, of giving all the police news all the time.[5]

It was Bennett, in 1868, who sent a reporter named Henry Morton Stanley to Africa to "find" the famous Scottish missionary Dr. David Livingstone—who was not actually lost. The reporter found him on the shore of Lake Tanganyika and said, "Dr. Livingstone, I presume?" Or so the story went. There were some who believed that Stanley never really got there. The reporter did not help his own claim when he said, "The public wants adventure rather than truth."

Finally, in the wave of invention that marked the end of the nineteenth century, the new steam-driven cylinder printing press made true mass circulation possible. For the first time, more than a few thousand readers along rail lines could get the news on the same day. Then came photography, telephone transmission, and wireless radio. But until World War II, it was considered a noteworthy achievement that a newsmagazine, *Time,* could be written in New York by Monday night of each week and be in homes everywhere in the country by Friday, four days later. "Every Tuesday a Near Miracle" was the headline over advertisements by the company that printed the magazine on Tuesdays, R. R. Donnelley and Sons of Chicago. This was how they said it in an ad in the February issue of *Fortune* magazine in 1934:

> Late Monday night. From Washington the President announces to a waiting nation his stupendous N.R.A. recovery program . . . Another Monday. Swollen with torrential rains and melting drifts from Tibetan passes, the terrible tiger-yellow Hwang Ho spreads a snarling flood roof-deep across Honan, drowns 50,000 . . . The small hours of a Tuesday morning. Far at sea a swirling, howling tempest crashes the *Akron* in sudden tragedy . . . A black Monday-Tuesday midnight. Pith helmeted British magistrates motor out from Ahmadabad, clap under arrest wizened, trouble-making St. Gandhi . . . And on Friday in the far corners of the United States, people read in a red-bordered magazine the dramatic, detailed stories of these events, stories intimate, accurate, minutely verified.

Studio television linked the country in the 1950s. But even in 1960, when the new president of the United States, John F. Kennedy, was asked what he considered the most important medium in the country, he answered: "*Time* magazine." Print's old dominance ended forever only with the development of live satellite television transmission. In 1975, the *Wall Street Journal* used the same technology to create the first true national newspaper, beaming page layouts to printing plants around the country. Next came the electronic means to store the knowledge of the world in a wired bit of ceramic biscuit and send that information almost instantaneously anywhere in the world.

Now the invention wave at the end of the twentieth century is creating individual media again—and just as surely foreshadowing great events. Communication by the Internet is beginning to make a mockery of repressive sedition laws around the world. New technologies come and go, rise and fall, sweeping all before them, kings and scribes alike—before they lose out to something else. Network television, once all-seen and all-powerful, is losing viewers and impact. Newspapers, in fact, seem to be in better long-range shape than television news. It may be better to know you are old than to be caught in the middle between the old and the new and not know which way to go.

Whether or not one agrees that the medium is the message, new or innovative technology continues to change the media, and the news as well. A couple of years ago, Sharp, a Japanese company, developed a hand-held video camera with a lens that rotated 360 degrees in a vertical plane, thus allowing users to film themselves at arm's length and see themselves at the same time on a small built-in television monitor. The metaphysics of the camera, priced at about $1,500, was post-Warhol and gave a new twist to his notion that electronic advances would translate into fifteen minutes of fame for everyone. The user of the Sharp camera could be both subject and producer, both story and storyteller.

There was nothing between the user-star-director and the camera—and the screen. No middleman. No filter. No editor, no reporter. A thirty-two-year-old public television producer in New York named Steven Rosenbaum built a show around the camera, selling his concept to MTV (Music Video Television) as *The UNfiltered News*. He gave young people video cameras and other equipment to tell their own stories. Soon hundreds were writing in each week, and Rosenbaum would pick one or two or ten that he thought might work as nonfiction entertainment. As you would expect, some of the *UNfiltered* segments were sophomoric, stupid, or self-indulgent—or all of the above. Like news. But some of them were both unique and powerful, including the self-filmed story of a heroin addict and a piece on breast cancer, in which a twenty-three-year-old named Tina Pavlou filmed her own mastectomy surgery and then her own chemotherapy sessions.

There is something symbolic in the fact that the man who created this show, Steven Rosenbaum, is a veritable timeline of journalism. His father was a printer, and his uncle Jerry Landay was once the White House correspondent for CBS News. Rosenbaum himself covered the New York State legislature for public television. He knows the difference between filtered and unfiltered news. Watching a segment made by a teenager on the suicide of a thirteen-year-old friend, Rosenbaum told the fourteen-year-old *auteur* that she never revealed how or why the friend had killed himself. "That's not important," she said. What she wanted to communicate was her own pain. That was her story; that was her journalism. He let her do it her way.

I spent some time hanging around Rosenbaum's operation,

BNN (Broadcast News Network), on lower Fifth Avenue in Manhattan. Young people, smart ones from smart colleges, who might have gone to the *New York Times* or NBC News, were tapping away at small consoles, mixing magic with images filmed or computer-created. At a showing of some of his work, done for CBS News, Rosenbaum said there would be a showing on Channel 280. I started to laugh, thinking that was a joke. No one else did. It turns out there is a Channel 280 on Direct-TV.

Back at BNN's headquarters, looking over hundreds of thousands of dollars' worth of blinking and bipping consoles and cameras, I asked Rosenbaum, "How long before this stuff is scrap in a junkyard?"

"Two years," he answered. Later he called me and said he had exaggerated. "The real figure is probably closer to eighteen months."

So little time, so much to do. In the process of writing a piece for the *New Yorker* magazine on President Clinton, I asked Vice-President Gore, for six years a reporter for the *Nashville Tennessean,* about the differences between the Washington he came to as a congressman in 1977 and the one Clinton came to in 1993. "The whole country is different," he said. "All these body blows to the sense of national well-being. The economic transformations . . . The disorienting effect of all this electronic information."

Then he added: "Do you know Prigogine's work?"

Ilya Prigogine is the father of chaos theory, a Belgian scientist (Russian-born) who won a Nobel Prize in 1977 for his work in defining "dissipative structures." Gore went on, "He proved that if you look at a system—say, a chamber—with

more and more energy and matter coming in, it will sponta-
neously reorganize itself into a more complicated system.
Something different will come out, but what it is can't be
predicted beforehand."

Pow! A Money-Information Complex instead of the old
Military-Industrial Complex. Public Opinion Democracy—
government of the polls, by the polls, and for the polls. Numbers make news. Money makes numbers. Three trillion dollars. Forty-eight percent. Polls are the new constituencies.
Fame is money. Reporters get more of both than the people
they cover. Everyone is the same size on television. One man
plus a fax becomes a majority. New men, new women, new
media, new money, new information, new relationships, new
sounds, new smells, new laws. Individualism morphs into
celebrity and so does lawmaking: "the Brady Bill," "Megan's
Law." Now an electronic beltway separates the chamber from
the nation.

The chamber is the capital city. Washington is information
driven now—or driven crazy by instant information. Decision making is high speed and interactive; the process of
analysis and adjustment is reactive and continuous. "News
cycles," which not so long ago meant information produced
to meet the needs of afternoon and morning newspapers and
then the evening network news, have exploded into something like a million car radios stuck on "Scan."

"These changes," said Gore," are not friendly to the linear
debate envisioned by the Founding Fathers."

Linear thought, in fact, may be a principal casualty of
these electronic times. Digital information and picture languages may not be very friendly to those of us who learned to

make a living on typewriters. Some of those who owned typewriters are ready to join the technological conquerors. If they can. This is from a memo sent to employees of the *Minneapolis Star-Tribune*, the nineteenth-largest paper in the country: "The goal is to change Minnesotans' perception of the *Star Tribune* from that of a newspaper to 'the brand of choice for information products.' . . . We need to move as far away as possible from the newspaper as the point of reference and focus on a product that's the most different from the newspaper . . . And work will be done to create a personality that is positive, contemporary, and appealing to our customers."[6]

Good luck. The fear or foresight behind that memo is everywhere in newsrooms, both print and electronic. John Haile of the Orlando paper said it this way: "I think that one of the real threats that we have to deal with is that we will end up being content providers for somebody else's business . . . They become the ones who would go out and aggregate the content, and put their brand on it."

Those words are part of the newspaper/Internet jargon. In a full-page advertisement that appeared in *Editor and Publisher* on February 14, 1998, a computer service selling to newspapers began its pitch this way: "You can surrender your city without a fight. Or . . . build traffic and revenue and block the Internet giants [with] everything from arts and entertainment guides, to automotive and real estate guides, to a Business Directory, community self-publishing services, editorial tools, and more."

Who is the enemy attacking newspapers from the Internet? The ad says Microsoft is offering such services in ten cities, *Yahoo!* in twelve cities, AOL in thirty-two. Then the copy ends: "Sooner or later, they'll have one in your market, too."

The biggest brander of them all these days, Bill Gates of Microsoft, tried to calm such fears at the 1997 convention of the Newspaper Association of America. "Don't think of Microsoft as a primary competitor here," he told publishing types. "We're not doing local news. We're not doing classified. We're seeing where this technology can go."[7]

"Part of this crowd may be gullible enough to buy that, but I do not," said Bob Ingle, vice-president of new media at Knight-Ridder, one of the country's biggest newspaper chains. A colleague, Heath Meriwether, publisher of the *Detroit Free Press,* said the same thing in webspeak: "Disingenuous.com."

One of the things Intel's Andy Grove told newsmen at ASNE in 1996 was: "You are going to be in a position like a lot of other people who have competed with a Microsoft and did not act aggressively enough . . . This happens one reader at a time, one viewer at a time, one article at a time . . . It is happening today."

Yes, it is. A Microsoft internal memo in December 1996 said: "We are challenging old and established businesses like newspapers, travel agencies, automobile dealers, entertainment guides, travel guides, Yellow Page directories, magazines, and over time many other areas . . . We must devise ways of working with them or winning away their customers and revenue streams . . . We must be aggressive."[8]

Whatever is happening, experience and history do show that people can wake up one morning and find their lives changed by something they had barely noticed. My favorite source on this subject is Jacqueline Goddard, who was a model for the photographer Man Ray in Paris in the late 1920s. The artists and writers she knew worked hard and believed in what they were doing. And they played hard, drinking and gossiping each night at La Coupole on the Boulevard Montparnasse, where they all went to pick up notes and messages left with a friendly bartender. Then one day it all ended. How? Goddard said, "It was the telephone. The telephone was the death of Montparnasse."

No one knows what must die now, but you can easily see which way things are going. Jerry Yang, the twenty-eight-year-old cofounder of *Yahoo!*, the Internet browser, was just out of graduate school at Stanford (in electrical engineering) when he and his roommate, David Filo, made more than a quarter of a billion dollars in the initial public offering of their little company. As I walked with Yang through *Yahoo!* headquarters, passing cluttered cubicles of surfers clicking away and away, looking for new and interesting websites, he said: "All of the stuff they're seeing is self-publishing, self-distributing—creating a new genre of content . . . It's irreversible, and it's incredibly democratizing. The technology is the least of it. It's social change. It has to be open, and it responds to demand. It's always on the edge."

If You Can't Beat 'Em, Buy 'Em

Someone who didn't much like a particular column by Richard Cohen of the *Washington Post* came up to him and said, "The trouble with you guys is that you're afraid of the president."

"No, we're not afraid of presidents," said Cohen. "What we're afraid of is Michael Eisner and Disney, Jack Welch of GE, Rupert Murdoch, John Malone, and whoever's running Westinghouse, and Mark Willes in Los Angeles."[1]

They own us, in one way or another. Eisner's company, Disney, owns ABC. General Electric owns NBC. Murdoch created his own television network, Fox, with money made by his newspapers around the world. Westinghouse, always chasing GE, owns CBS. Malone runs TCI, a cable conglomerate that uses its power over allocation of channels in hundreds of cities to push around—some might say shake down—networks and programmers. On a smaller patch, the U.S. Virgin Islands, the owner of the islands' telephone company, Jeffrey Prosser, got tired of seeing the *Virgin Island Daily News* attack his company's pricing policies and a certain corporate arrogance. In September 1997, he bought the paper from the Gannett chain for $17 million. Somewhere along the line, mogul instinct or smart public relations lieutenants came up with the oldest and best way to handle a frustrating press corps: If you can't beat them, buy them![2]

That is the way it has usually worked in the history of communications. The young and the edgy, like Jerry Yang and David Filo, begin a process that ends with takeover and control by the usual suspects, the established and rich. Individuals create; organizations control. Or as Yang's contemporaries might say: Organizations rule! Instead of suffering the slings and arrows of independent press reports dealing with price-fixing investigations and cheating on defense contracts, a company like GE can mobilize its own power and wealth to help shape a new kind of business press. Financial reporters can be replaced by stock analysts, whose analysis is free (if self-serving), linking journalism and investment banking in efficient, one-stop shopping. Business-leaning economists can come forward to tell viewers and readers that high unemployment is now good news—just the right thing to help American companies compete in the global marketplace.

Mark Willes does not own the Times-Mirror Company, but he manages it with what appears to be total power—and faith that what the press needs is less journalism and more marketing. "The Numbers" make me do it, he says to anyone who will listen: overall newspaper circulation has declined 10 percent over the past twelve years; the share of local advertising in newspapers has declined from 57 percent to 47 percent over the past twenty years; from 1991 to 1997, the *Los Angeles Times*'s circulation dropped more than 200,000 from a peak of 1,242,000. Another number he uses is 6,200, the number of Times-Mirror jobs he eliminated in his first year. Willes took a few himself, assuming a range of titles, from chairman of the parent company to publisher of its flagship paper, the *Los Angeles Times*. The smaller ships of the Times-Mirror fleet include the *Baltimore Sun, Newsday* on Long Island, and the *Hartford Courant*. Willes came to Times-Mirror in 1995 and announced his presence by closing down *New York Newsday,* the Long Island paper's classy city edition, and the money-losing Washington edition of the *Los Angeles Times*. (The latter decision was quickly reversed after complaints by California's congressional delegation, proving there is still some power in old-fashioned politics.)

The list could go on, and it does. Sixty-two people on the *Forbes* magazine list of the four hundred richest men and women in America are in some sort of "media" or "entertainment" business. Harry Evans, a former editor of the *Sunday Times* in London, who brought his talents to book publishing and journalism in New York, offered this bit of sad wisdom after working for Rupert Murdoch: "The challenge of American newspapers is not to stay in business—it is to stay in journalism."[3]

Murdoch and Willes would argue that without good business there would be no journalism. Whatever our virtues, journalists are cantankerous employees. We are deft advocates for our own self-interest, ever poised to project any disagreement with management as a struggle between godly "public service" (ours) and evil "profit" (theirs). In 1890, writing in a Boston magazine called *The Arena,* W. H. H. Murray said he had an idea about how to save "honorable and right thinking journalism." The idea was to endow newspapers like universities. Eliminating owners was the only way to go, he said: "Money has no conscience, no honor, no patriotism, no sympathy with truth, right, and decency, and never has had."[4]

Truth, right, and decency—there we are! That is how Will Irwin, one of the great journalists of his day, wrote about it for *Collier's* in his 1911 series "The American Newspaper." The promotion for the fourteen articles began: "We have tried to take the broad view of journalism . . . The series is alive with interest, for we are dealing with the most romantic calling of modern times."

Yes!

Irwin, a star of the *New York Sun* in its greatest days, was a romantic himself—like the rest of us. He was paid $320 for each part of the *Collier's* series, turned down a $5,000 bribe from one publisher, and was sued for $500,000 by William Randolph Hearst after he wrote that the publisher of the *San Francisco Examiner* and the *New York Journal* was dealing in "the coin of the gutter." Specifically, Irwin showed that Hearst papers exchanged favorable editorial copy for theater advertisements.

And present not long after the creation of our rather young business, he advanced the lovely and anticapitalist notion that the man with the pen had more power than the man with the press and purse.

"What now of the reporter, the newest arm of this newest power in civilization?" he wrote. "Here is a young man sent out among the million complexities of the day to find the facts which will interest his world, to see truth for the homestayers, as truth presents itself to his point of view."

He quoted Charles A. Dana, the editor of the *New York Sun*, who said of the reporter: "He wields the real power of the press."

Yes! The cover of the April 22, 1911, issue of *Collier's*, which carried the seventh article in the series, showed reporters hovering, angel-like, over scurrying crooks, bankers, and other ne'er-do-wells.

Irwin couldn't stop himself: "The publisher alone, however, will never wholly reform the greater abuses of journalism. The impetus must come from the actual journalist, writing upstairs while the proprietor sells his wares downstairs, and from us, the public; not from the middleman, but from the producer and consumer."

He helped establish a lively precedent for newspapermen biting the hands that feed them: "When the newspaper is owned by a stock company, when its directors meet but to shave this year's expenses and increase next year's dividends, . . . the height of its policy is then enlightened selfishness . . . When the American Newspaper Publishers Association meets in national convention, it does not discuss methods of newsgathering nor editorial problems. The addresses treat with the price of white paper, of new machinery, of organization for extending circulation, of the advertising rate."[5]

Irwin was no radical, but he was a good enough observer and quickly got to the heart of the matter: "The 'system' in the American newspaper proceeds from the fact that the subscriber, who buys the newspaper that it may teach him about his times and fight his battles against privilege, is not paying for the newspaper. The advertisers are paying—about one percent united, in the present condition of American society, with the powers most dangerous to the common weal."[6]

Where that money comes from has been a critical factor in the history and development of the American newspaper business. The customer may not always be right, but he is usually catered to. Mass newspapers which made their money from many readers and few advertisers ran to bloody headlines and popular sensationalism—like the *National Enquirer* and the tabloid *Globe* today. Competitors with pages of respectable advertising and smaller circulations reflected the tastes of the "better" classes—like the *New York Times* and *Chicago Tribune* of today.

(Network television news is another matter. For most of its history, network news was a government-mandated supplement to advertiser-financed entertainment. Circulation was "free" and almost total, the masses converging on lowest-common-denominator entertainment.)

Real mass papers, the ones depending on and entertaining the masses rather than what used to be known as the "carriage trade," were not part of the "system." That is still true: the modern blood-and-sex tabloids, the ones in your face at the supermarket checkout counter, usually weeklies, carry very little advertising but are checked out by many, many readers.

Irwin's *Collier's* article on journalistic ethics included a photo with the caption, "News photographers waiting for their prey." He wrote: "The chief business for the true yellow journalist is to find the class of news which will interest the greatest number of people; and to this end, yellow journalism has made a formula: 'Sport for the men, love and scandal for the women.'" An executive of the Scripps chain of twenty-two newspapers had elaborated on that theme, telling

Irwin: "Money and politics for the men, love for the women,
. . . Power is a man's business, his chief intellectual liking;
politics, wealth and sport are all different manifestations of it.
Affection is a woman's business; love is affection at its height;
scandal is affection gone wrong."

And because of the nature of news, publishing and broadcasting companies have always had far greater political clout
than other enterprises of similar size. That is one of the
reasons Mr. Murdoch welcomed himself to America by buy-
ing the bad numbers but better political clout of the *New
York Post.* In 1911, the same year Will Irwin was dissecting
the business in *Collier's,* a congressional investigation turned
up this telegram to editors around the country from Herman
Ridder, the president of the American Newspaper Publishers
Association:

> New York, February 17, 1911
> By Request: Private to editors:
> It is of vital importance to newspapers that their Washington
> correspondents be instructed to treat favorably the Canadian
> reciprocity agreement, because print paper and wood pulp are
> made free of duty by this agreement.[7]

(Ridder's name, incidentally, lives on in the name of the
Knight-Ridder newspaper chain. The congressman in charge
of the 1911 investigation that turned up Ridder's telegram
was Charles A. Lindbergh, a Minnesota progressive whose
son Charles Jr., the aviator, probably sold more newspapers
than Knight-Ridder ever did.)

Another facet of the basic relationship between journalists
and their paychecks was defined in 1968 by Murray Kemp-

ton, then a *New York Post* columnist, in a review of *The Kingdom and the Power,* Gay Talese's book about the *New York Times.* He noted that some of the characters in the book were complaining about it, including *Times* managing editor Clifton Daniel and assistant managing editor A. M. Rosenthal. "Why are they angry?" asked Kempton, as I remember that column. "Without the attention this book gave them, they would be what they have always been: slaves of the rather pleasant young man who inherited them."

The young man who had inherited power at the *New York Times* in the 1960s was Arthur "Punch" Sulzberger, who operated within a family context which pledged that whatever else happened, the mission of the *New York Times* was to be the best newspaper in the world. One of the reasons he could do that and pass the company on to his son, Arthur Jr., in 1997 was that the family controlled the voting stock of the Times Company. By then, most of the other major American news operations, prodded by increasingly aggressive corporate owners and shareholders, had gone outside family, company, and journalism for pleasant and unpleasant managers whose primary obligation was not sharing the word but boosting the shares. Thus, in the late 1980s, according to *Editor and Publisher* magazine and other industry sources, the percentage of newspaper company revenues going into news operations dropped from 20 percent to about 7 percent.

That helped raise profits at most places, but not so much in Los Angeles. So Mark Willes came from General Mills, the food company, with a mandate to increase Times-Mirror's 10 percent annual profit, which might be considered high in most American businesses but was low compared with that of other sellers of journalism. In the last quarter of 1997, the average profit of newspaper companies was 21.3 percent. At Times-Mirror, operating profit doubled from the previous year to 21.2 percent. As that was happening, Willes' layoffs of employees were earning him the whispered office nickname "the Cereal Killer." Actually, though, Willes was not a world-class downsizer when compared to, say, Laurence Tisch, the hotel and tobacco mogul who reduced the staff of CBS News by one-third in little more than a year after his takeover—squeezing enough fat and blood out to leave both CBS and CBS News mere shells of what they had once been.

Whatever was said behind his back, Willes did what he was hired to do, doubling the value of Times-Mirror stock in just two years—and quieting down the three hundred members of the company's founding family, the Chandlers, who were living off stock dividends.[8] He was more interested in shareholder value than the pious values of journalists—for instance, the venerable church-state wall separating the editorial and business sides of news operations.

"I have suggested strongly and repeatedly that the people in the newsroom need to know and understand the people in our advertising department," Willes said early on. "There has been more than one person who has pointed out the wall between the newsroom and the advertising department. And every time they point it out, I get out a bazooka and tell them if they don't take it down, I'm going to blow it up."[9]

To make his point, he named business managers for each section of his *Los Angeles Times*—"News," "Sports," "Arts," and so on—with responsibility for making each a "profit center." In other words, sections like "Sports" and "Business" were being reorganized to turn a profit, or at least pay for themselves. Less advertising revenue, less news. The new order at the *Los Angeles Times* looked like the structure at General Mills, which has separate managers for Cheerios and other company brands. That seemed logical to Willes, and it probably is if you view newspapers as just another product to be marketed. The problem he faced is that those cantankerous or ignorant men and women of journalism prefer to think that selling scribbling is the single glorious exception to the rule that business is the business of America.

It is, for example, hard to imagine any other modern business that would allow two junior employees to put the corporation at risk by attacking the most powerful interests in the country, beginning with the president of the United States—all the while refusing to tell their bosses and owners what they were doing. But that, on a fundamental level, is exactly the story of Watergate and the Washington Post Company. Bob Woodward, the discoverer of the anonymous source he called "Deep Throat," had been with the company all of nine months, and he refused to tell editors who the source was.

A 1990s publisher—say, Mark Willes—would be expected to ask: "What the hell are you two talking about? What the hell do you think you're doing out there?"

Journalism. Woodward and Bernstein were doing journalism.

That's the press. An unusual trade, to say the least—forever raising a shield of exceptionalism rooted in the First Amendment of the Constitution and the liberalized libel precedents of the 1960s. An anomaly all these years. Now, with a different order of managers, it could become an anachronism. There may be a lesson here: journalism schools should be teaching and giving degrees in not only readin' and writin', but in the 'rithmetic of newsroom management. On our side too, if you can't beat the bosses, join 'em. Become a boss.

In terms of both our bosses and our government, I have always been amazed at how much we—journalists—get away with. In my heart, I believed something Ithiel de Sola Pool, a political scientist from the Massachusetts Institute of Technology, wrote years ago: "No nation will indefinitely tolerate a free press that serves to divide the country and to open the floodgates of criticism against the freely chosen government that leads it . . . If the press is the government's enemy, it is the free press that will end up being destroyed."

But so far, so good. The most serious attack on the legal independence of the American press came early in the history of the republic. Fearful of a war with France in 1798, Congress passed the Alien and Sedition Laws, setting punishment of up to two years in prison for any citizen who "shall write, print, utter, or publish . . . false, scandalous, and malicious writing against the government of the United States, or either House of the Congress of the United States, or the President of the United States." Several editors were imprisoned or fined. But the law lasted only two years before it was eliminated in 1800.

Still, we do glance over our shoulder at the powers and passions that be, choosing to communicate with words like "adversary" and "objective." We are a very odd bunch, uncertain with power and uneasy with what we thought when we were younger, standing in the back thinking we were the front. Anthony Trollope caught more than a little of that a while ago, in his 1855 novel *The Warden*. He describes, in delicious prose, a character named Tom Towers, editor of the *Daily Jupiter:*

> He loved to watch the great men of whom he daily wrote, and flatter himself that he was greater than any of them. Each of them was responsible to his country, each of them must answer if inquired into, each of them must endure abuse with good humour, and insolence without anger. But to whom was he, Tom Towers, responsible? No one could insult him; no one could inquire into him . . . Ministers courted him, though perhaps they knew not his name. Bishops feared him; judges doubted their own verdicts unless he confirmed; and generals, in their councils of war, did not consider more deeply what the enemy would do than what the *Jupiter* would say . . . It was possible that Tom Towers considered himself the most powerful man in Europe. And so he walked on day-to-day studiously striving to look like a man, but knowing within his breast that he was a god.

Six decades later, in his *Spoon River Anthology*, Edgar Lee Masters offered an American take on the arrogance of the press. In blank verse, Editor Whedon is made to say:

To be able to see every side of every question;
To be on every side, to be everything, to be nothing long;
. . . To wear a mask like the Greek actors—
Your eight-page paper—behind which you huddle,
Bawling through the megaphone of big type:
"This is I, the giant."

All of that is still true, even as editors are being pushed around now by the aggressive new top-down bottom-line management of our day—and these are crisis years, as readership and viewer numbers decline. One editor after another has fallen or been pushed out, basically for insubordination in the face of financial managers. Some casualties were prominent, men considered to be among the best in the business: James Squires of the *Chicago Tribune,* Eugene Roberts and James Naughton of the *Philadelphia Inquirer,* Bill Kovach of the *Atlanta Journal-Constitution,* and Shelby Coffee III, under Willes at the *Los Angeles Times.* Others were less well known but just as disillusioned and frustrated.

Tom White, the fifty-one-year-old editor of the *Lincoln Star Journal* in Nebraska, quit in April 1997, writing to his corporate superiors at Lee Enterprises in Davenport, Iowa: "I have concluded that the company's emphasis on increasing profits and centralization, its contradictory initiatives and its frenetic, hard-boiled culture, which is often out-of-touch with its employees, are subverting the complex craft of community journalism, from which this company's very business once sprung."[10]

In the early 1990s David Burgin, the former editor of the *Houston Post,* put it this way: "I don't think editors are as good or as powerful as they were ten or fifteen years ago. The new power in the industry is the marketing director. I want to see more swashbuckling editors like Ben Bradlee or Jim Bellows. But those days are dead. Now it's target marketing and target marketing and more marketing."[11]

The current struggle between bosses and journalists in newsrooms across the country is basic. They are fighting over what is news and how much it's worth to go out and get it. Steve Crosby, editor of the *Wausau Daily Herald* in Wisconsin, spoke for new management most everywhere when he said, "News is what our readers say it is."[12]

So papers are painting over their window on the world, choosing to hold up a mirror to their audience. The *Wausau Daily Herald* got rid of two of its three reporters covering city and county government—and larger newspapers and television networks have done the same and more to reduce foreign coverage. Polls and focus groups and whims are being used to create a profitable little tyranny of the majority of readers or viewers.

Journalism was never art, certainly not science, and would be hard to call a profession. But whatever it was, it excited the people in it. From the tribe's perspective, the "product" was not a product because it was different every day, indeed every hour. It was also a way of life, like farming. New managers reject that kind of romanticism and are doing their best to quantify such notions out of existence.

In Winston-Salem, North Carolina, the *Journal* talked productivity up front, setting goals or quotas for stories designated by letters and numbers. That reform was developed by productivity consultants, whose work was analyzed and published by the *University of North Carolina Journalist*. Here are two examples:

> An A-1 story should be six inches or less. A reporter should use a press release and/or one or two "cooperative sources." He or she should take 0.9 hours to do each story and should be able to produce forty of those in a week.

A B-3 story should come from a longer event and/or some uncooperative sources. It should be six inches to twelve inches, and the ideal reporter should churn out seven of them per week.[13]

Those proposed rules were subverted and rejected by *Journal* editors and reporters, but such ideas are alive and growing. Working for the Project for Excellence in Journalism, a company called Princeton Survey Research Associates examined 1,565 statements and allegations made during a week in February 1998 by major newspapers, network television news operations, and even news-talk shows, including ABC News's *Nightline* and PBS's *Charlie Rose Show*. The predictable conclusion was that such outfits were producing less and less "news" and more and more "analysis." Then the Princeton group reported: "Looked at another way, the picture that emerges is of a news culture that is increasingly involved with disseminating information rather than gathering it."

In other words: fewer reporters, more profits. Whether or not journalism declines into just another business, a wonderfully profitable one for owners. The ATM news scenario could complement computerized radio stations.The government, corporations, and public relations types will be able to deposit or withdraw news anytime day or night in a slot at the front of the building. In the back, consumers could punch up whatever they fancied. There would be no need for human beings inside the building—if you consider reporters human beings.

To be more specific (if more anecdotal) than Princeton

researchers, here's an example of what I mean. Comparing notes with a young man reporting on Congress for midwestern chain newspapers, I realized that his job was, in a fundamental way, exactly the opposite of mine when I was his age. At the *New York Times* in the 1970s, if editors saw you in the city room in the middle of the day, they would ask, "Hey, Reeves, how come you're not out working on stories?" Now, if my modern counterpart was not at his terminal, he would be asked later, "Where were you?" If he answered, "I was at the Capitol, talking with Senator X," his bosses would want to know why he couldn't do that by e-mail.

One more thing, obvious but significant. At the *New York Times* in those old days, I could and did go out on assignments for an hour, a day, a week, and come back and say, "There's no story." Where productivity rules, when they send you out on a B-3, they want a B-3 and they want it now. If you can't do it, they'll find someone else—that's why high unemployment is management's friend.

Reporters don't have as many friends. Left to their own instincts, reporters look for trouble. We are often used and often despised, but such things rarely intrude on the chase after lies and meanness and sham—so that presidents and governors and mayors and ordinary citizens can decide what to do about such things. We are out there ready to save the world, whether it wants to be saved or not. It is a job for young people.

On the business side of the wall, where news is what they put between the advertising or the commercials, the marketeers must often think reporters are nuts—or, worse, corporate-destructive. The uneasy relationship between newsrooms and counting-rooms is not helped by the fact that reporters have traditionally been ignorant and hostile when it comes to reporting or even talking about business and economics. Gretchen Morgensen, who served as magazine publisher Steve Forbes's press secretary during his 1996 run for the Republican nomination for president, got it about right when she said, "America's political reporters just don't care to understand even the simplest economic concepts . . . I mean the basics, like supply and demand, or the effects of taxation on economic growth and personal savings."[14]

The business types in news organizations have their blind spots, too, to the point that they seem convinced there is a cause-and-effect relationship between hours at the terminal and story length and quality. Increased revenues and cost-cutting are their games: they want fewer reporters writing more words on subjects that please readers. In other words, give readers and viewers less on government and more on suburban lifestyles. A penny saved, a penny earned. In the spring of 1997 I was shocked when a *New York Times* "correspondent" named Julia Campbell was arrested for disorderly conduct after she swore at cops during the funeral, in Brooklyn, of a young rap singer named "Notorius B.I.G." What shocked me was not her words—"You bastards!"—but the fact that Ms. Campbell was a "stringer," not a real correspondent with health benefits and all that. Has it come to this, I thought—New York City's dominant paper "out-sourcing" coverage of Brooklyn? Yes, it has. The *Times, Time* magazine, and CBS News used to argue that the only way to guarantee credibility was to use only your own people. No more, not if news subcontractors are cheaper.

And then the *Times* apologized to the police. Through assistant counsel George Freeman the paper declared: "We have to look beyond the individual incident to the continuum of dealing with the police department. To be antagonistic would not serve us in the long run."[15]

The *Times* changes. Brooklyn news is not worth a full-time reporter, and backing up part-time reporters is not worth upsetting the police. When I was working for the paper, we upset the police plenty, particularly by investigating and publishing the corruption charges brought to us by a couple of young cops named David Durk and Frank Serpico.

There was a time when great news organizations would fight police departments, and libel suits, too, as a matter of principle. But to the cool business heads moving into newsrooms, it is a matter of capital—fighting most suits makes no economic sense to them. Besides, juries are showing a tendency to see the press as part of the money-bagged establishment, delivering verdicts that give plaintiffs hundreds of millions of dollars for real or imagined damages caused by reporters doing their jobs. Publish and be damned is becoming publish and be deposed—or sold out by the boss's lawyers.

The field has tilted away from journalism values to business dogma. Now even a tiny country like Singapore can push around the greatest of American press operations. Lee Kuan Yew, the country's founding father, has collected millions of dollars in libel judgments and settlements paid by the *New York Times* and *Washington Post* because the country's first families do not like being criticized by foreigners in the *International Herald Tribune,* jointly owned by the *Post* and *Times*. Paying is the easy way. So are popular television news segments with demipopulist titles like "The Fleecing of America," yelling that Washington is taking "Your Money." The producers choose their targets with care—because, again, government does not sue, but corporations do.

Even in corporate harness, most journalists are tribal. Loyalty to paycheck does not always diminish the call of drums and pipes faraway. There was an interesting show of that in New York City in October 1997, at a black-tie night at the Waldorf-Astoria Hotel. The occasion was the annual dinner of the Committee to Protect Journalists, an organization that monitors and aids reporters jailed or violently harassed around the world. That is, the survivors. Twenty-seven journalists were murdered or killed in action in 1997.

The dinner was chaired by one of the men Dick Cohen says we are afraid of: Michael Eisner, the chairman of Disney, who that night was in costume as the boss of ABC News. Eisner rambled on about how much he had learned about journalism in the television and movie business. The applause was polite, barely. The speaker understood neither the subject nor the audience.

The final speaker was an ABC News cast member, Ted Koppel of *Nightline*. He was prepared, reading from a text, a gesture which the audience took as a symbol that he cared, that he understood what he was saying and meant it:

> We celebrate tonight the men and women whose dedication to the collection and distribution of facts threatens their very existence. When they antagonize those with money, political power and guns, they risk their lives. We, on the other hand, tremble at nothing quite so much as the thought of boring our

audiences . . . The preferred weapons of the rich and powerful here in America are the pollster and the public relations counsel. But they are no threat to the safety of journalists.

Our enemies are far more insidious than that. They are declining advertising revenues, the rising costs of newsprint, lower ratings, diversification, and the vertical integration of communications empires. They are breezier, chattier styles of insinuating themselves onto the front pages of our more distinguished newspapers. They are the fading lines between television news and entertainment . . . It is not death, or torture, or imprisonment that threatens us as American journalists; it is the trivialization of our industry.[16]

"The Tribe"

I made it to New York not long after politicians stopped
calling us "the Boys"—as in, "Bring in the Boys!" The name
put reporters in their place, socially and economically. There
were exceptions, of course. Half the reporters at the *New York
Times* seemed to be former editors of the *Harvard Crimson* or
the *Yale Daily News,* but even at the *Times* most newspapermen were the same kind of men who became cops. Street-
smart Irishmen and Jews, storytellers who had started as
copy boys. Their lives were more interesting than most, but
generally they were not paid particularly well, and many had
not finished college—if they'd ever started.

Like the four-W's lead ("Who, what, where, and when?"),
the idea of "reporters" came with the telegraph. By the end of
the nineteenth century, James Gordon Bennett's ideas of sys-
tematic news-gathering had gone from radical to traditional.
In 1897 Lincoln Steffens could write, "It is pretty generally
accepted now that a newspaper has to print the news . . .
Even the old organs of class and political prejudices, which
rely for their standing upon their editorial and literary articles, find it necessary to keep up a news service."[1]

"News" had triumphed over opinion. Reporting was a job description—and a generally stimulating means of support. In news, the world is made new every . . . well, it used to be every day. Now, or soon, it will be every minute, every second. Mickey Carroll, the *Trib* guy who got me to New York, used to say he could not imagine a better life than being a general-assignment reporter for a morning newspaper: come in at eleven o'clock each day, without knowing where you'll be going; meet new people; see new things; write about them with your name on top; go home at seven for dinner, with a head cleared and empty—until the new world of tomorrow.

Television correspondents do something like that, but having one's face on camera may be headier stuff than just a byline. I have seen grown and famous men cry in the field when they heard back from headquarters that their story had been killed or shortened—they'd get no face time that night. The deepest fault line in the geography of press standards is self-censorship: reporters and correspondents generally give editors and owners what they want, because what they want is what they print or show.

It has been that way for a long time. Journalists seem always to have defined themselves and the business by looking back to romance long gone. There is an entire literature by reporters complaining about changes, always bad, from the old days—when they were young. I take those recurring complaints as the insecure suspicion of tribal elders—Katz's "Old Farts"—that young braves may be smarter than the grayheads. Whether this is true or not, the young are more likely to do what they are told and to deliver what is expected.

H. L. Mencken, the caustic sage of Baltimore, was born in 1869 but seemed to have the same newsroom experience I did, writing in the *Baltimore Evening Sun* of January 10, 1927: "A good reporter used to make as much as a bartender or a police sergeant; he now makes as much as the average doctor or lawyer, and probably a great deal more . . . He is no longer a free-lance in human society, thumbing his nose at its dignitaries . . . The highest sordid aspiration that any reporter had, in my time, was to own two complete suits of clothes. Today they have dinner coats."²

In 1927 Silas Bent, a former *New York Times* reporter, was outraged when the *Times* gave as much headline space to the Dempsey-Tunney heavyweight championship fight as it had given to the end of World War I in 1918. He wrote the following in a book titled *Ballyhoo:*

> Even at the risk of provoking the reproach that I am casting unmerited glamor over "the good old days," I must insist that the legend of the reporter as a picturesque and adventurous figure, however persistently maintained in newspaper offices as a present-day actuality, is but a legend . . . Now, when high-speed machinery has reduced the beat to a matter, say, of an hour, at the end of which competing newspapers are on the street with the same story, . . . reporters seldom strive for it. Instead, they work in squads. They interview celebrities in groups. The only rivalry left to them lies in the effort to get more space and display for the same material.³

That was in 1927. In 1997 Pete Hamill, then the editor of the *New York Daily News,* said this: "Careerists began to dominate craftsmen in all areas of American life; it wasn't enough to carve leather into a perfect shoe; you must also long to run the shoe company . . . If you had a hot raw talent from a junior college, or a high-school drop-out, how could he or she get a chance before someone with a degree from Stanford? . . . I am now a proud member of a craft that today would not grant me entry."[4]

So perhaps there really is nothing new under the sun—or the *Chronicle,* the *Times,* or CNN. That is how we have always seen ourselves—not as solid citizens, but as adventurers on deadline. The thrill is a thing inside ourselves, not a reaction to outside forces or events or environments. From the telegraph to the telephone to "Intel Inside," journalists sound the same, say the same things. If such minds are flexible, new technologies—the Internet, for one—will be appropriated by local and regional news organizations to recreate the updated and salable around-the-clock excitement of "Extra! Read all about it!"

Silas Bent had this to say about why journalists thrive on perpetual novelty: "There is acute personal aggrandizement. One derives the satisfaction which Mrs. Galewski experiences when she passes to a neighbor a fresh tidbit of gossip. One experiences the joy, on more momentous occasions, which must have been Paul Revere's when, as a sort of morning newspaper extra, he made the midnight ride to Lexington. So long as the tribe of reporters persists, this must be its chief reward. This is the sure excitement for which he barters his time and energies."[5]

How, then, do these brothers and sisters across time define news? One of the first determined attempts to answer that question was Will Irwin's series in *Collier's.* Published in 1911, it was billed as the complete word on "the whole subject of American journalism—the most powerful extrajudicial force in society, except religion."[6]

Irwin, who covered the 1906 San Francisco earthquake for the *New York Sun,* wrote of the experience five years later in *Collier's:*

> News is the main thing . . . It is both an intellectual craving and a commercial need to the modern world. In popular psychology, it has come to be a crying primal want of the mind, like hunger of the body . . . Most dramatically the San Francisco disaster illuminated this point. On the morning of April 20, 1906, the city's population huddled in parks and squares, the houses gone, death from famine or thirst a rumor and a possibility . . .
>
> When, at dawn, the paper was printed . . . they had to drive at top speed, casting out the sheets as they went, to make any progress at all. No bread wagon, no supply of blankets, caused half so much stir as did the arrival of news. We need, we crave it; this nerve of the modern world transmits thought and impulse from the brain of humanity to its muscles; the complex organism of modern society could no more move without it than a man could move without filament and ganglia.
>
> A million billion things occur hourly in the world, from the movement of the finger by which I write this line to the surging of the crowd which is at this minute harrying strike-breakers along the Canadian border. The movement of this finger is not news, while the surge of that crowd is . . . Here lies the distinction and it is also a definition: The beating of strike-breakers is news because it is a departure from the established order . . .
>
> That mankind will consume an undue amount of news about crime and disorder is only a proof that the average human being is optimistic; that he believes the world to be true, sound, and working upward. Crimes and scandals interest him most because they most disturb his picture of the established order.

Irwin also quoted, approvingly, a sort of definition by a reporter named Tiffany Blake: "Most news is not fact at all. It is gossip about facts."

"In this," Irwin wrote, "I think he has said a wise and final word . . . News is the impressionistic picture of truth. It is gossip organized to our uses, subdued to our hand, and raised to both a science and an art. For before journalism was, the town or tribal gossip discharged in irregular and primitive fashions."

The established order may be more complex today than it was in primitive times, or in 1911. There are more news delivery systems and more cynical definitions, including this one from 1998 by a *New York Post* gossip columnist named Neil Travis: "Gossip is journalism today, and we professional gossips are being pushed further back in the paper. That bothers me, because gossip is too important to be left to amateurs."

"It's a simple business . . . not exactly rocket-scientist stuff." This is a quote from Michael Bloomberg, who stumbled into the news business—or the business news business. When he created Bloomberg Business News in 1992, he thought he was in the data and information business, selling up-to-the-second numbers to money managers who could afford to lease his computer terminals for $1,500 a month. Five years later he was hiring reporters and editors and opening sixty-seven bureaus around the world. Why hire real reporters? "I needed their judgment," he said, echoing Bill Keller of the *New York Times*.[7]

Then Bloomberg added that the hard part was gritting his teeth and backing up the news side, even when his reporters were putting out news hurting his clients—the companies which were paying him that $1,500 a month per terminal. But it was the judgment of people who called themselves reporters and editors that gave him the thing he needed most: credibility.

There are something like 120,000 journalists in the United States, about one-third of them women. The most important fact about them is that they are getting old and do not make very much money. The average age of these men and women is thirty-seven or thirty-eight, with television journalists generally five years younger than print people. Fifteen years ago the average age of all journalists, print and electronic, was thirty-two. Nearly half the men and women working on newspapers now are older than forty, compared with about a fourth just eight years ago. Only 4 percent of newspaper journalists are under twenty-five, compared with 12 percent in the 1970s and 1980s. The starting salaries of journalists, print and electronic, are between $15,000 and $25,000—far lower than those of professional groups—lower than those of tolltakers on the New Jersey Turnpike, for that matter. The average salary for all journalists, including the few multi-million-dollar television stars, is about $31,000.[8] (To give some perspective here: According to the *Los Angeles Times* of January 18, 1988, there are 312,000 people in the entertainment business in Los Angeles County alone; they earn an average of $62,000 a year. Jersey Turnpike tolltakers are paid $28,300–$41,600 a year, plus overtime.)

These are pretty light numbers, particularly for people supposed to be all-powerful in a country where money is the most common yardstick of value and influence. The "power of the press" seems even less formidable if you read surveys of readers and viewers of news. Two-thirds of Americans over the age of fifty say that keeping up with the news is "very important" to them; but only about 40 percent of Americans under thirty say the same thing. That is the formula for Andy Grove's demographic time bomb.[9]

The aging of journalists is no small thing to a practitioner. There have never been large numbers of old reporters. In their mid-thirties and early forties, many men and women in the business face up-or-out situations: become a boss, a deputy editor of some kind, or move on. Daily reporting, print or electronic, is a business of strong legs and a certain naïveté. Not everyone sees the world made new every twenty-four hours—or every hour. Cynicism hits the street on weak legs. Even Will Irwin, our romantic star, had moments of great self-doubt about his chosen line of work. He became depressed while covering the peace conference which ended the Russo-Japanese War, in August 1905, at Portsmouth, New Hampshire. His biographer, Robert V. Hudson, wrote:

> He was feeling desperate about being stuck in journalism . . . He discovered he was much more like the typical reporter than he had ever suspected. On the surface the reporters were pleasant, witty perhaps, magnetic in talk, and artists at telling stories orally. Together they were overly merry, yet underneath their congeniality was a sadness, a persistent haunting melancholy and a sense of failure, a fear of the future, a hatred of life . . . Liquored up, one might confess that he was trying to get out of journalism but could not and probably never could.[10]

But, ironically, if the business is now in decline, the new Will Irwins, the stars and celebrities among us, are often better paid and a good deal more famous than the people they cover. "We all know how it works," said David Gergen, who certainly does. The magazine editor, television commentator, and counselor to presidents put it this way: "You write something provocative enough to get on television, then you say something even more provocative on television, and then you make the big money on lecture dates around the country."[11]

Flying to a lecture date not long ago, I picked up the magazine in the seat pocket in front of me: *USAir Magazine,* which is published by a division of the *New York Times.* I came across an advertisement promoting a feature called "Coming Home," in which "some of today's best-known personalities" write or are interviewed about where they come from or where they live now. Twelve of the nineteen celebrities featured in the ad were journalists. The list was headed, alphabetically, by actors Lauren Bacall and Kenneth Branagh. Then, in the same order, came Art Buchwald, Katie Couric, Michael Kinsley, Jane Pauley, George Plimpton, Anna Quindlen, Cokie Roberts, Tim Russert, Diane Sawyer, Gloria Steinem, Gay Talese, George Will.

Fame is a useful weapon for a journalist. It is not hard to imagine the so-called kids in the Clinton White House (presidencies have always been fueled by the sleepless energy of young overachievers) calling home to tell Mom and Dad, "You're not going to believe who I talked to today: Cokie Roberts!" When Bob Woodward let it be known in 1993 that he wanted to write a book on the first year of the Clinton presidency, the president himself told his assistants that they should give Woodward whatever he wanted—as if that were their patriotic duty. (Woodward's book, *The Agenda: Inside the Clinton White House,* was published in 1994. One of its interesting revelations was that political consultants expert at press relations, specifically James Carville and Paul Begala, appeared to have equal status with the secretary of the treasury and economists at White House meetings on economic policy.)

The *New York Times* had no regard for celebrity newsmen when I was there in the 1970s. Reporters were generally prohibited from appearing on television. Now the good, gray lady has a public relations agent trying to get her reporters on television shows. With good reason. Television exposure makes reporters more desirable leaking-partners for sources.

This is Anthony Lake, President Clinton's national security adviser during his first term, answering a question from me about changes in the press: "When I first came here, in the Nixon White House, if you wanted to know what a reporter really thought about the people and issues he covered you had to get drunk with him. Maybe a couple of times. Now I just turn on television to find out what they think."

That same night, I turned on *The Capital Gang*, a Cable News Network show; and, sure enough, there was Al Hunt, the *Wall Street Journal's* Washington editor, telling Mississippi senator Trent Lott that he expected him to vote for GATT (the General Agreement on Tariffs and Trade) for the good of the country. And Lott was analyzing the news of the day and asking questions of the gang of four reporters. The world turned upside down.

"Say 'Hi' to your mom," said Hunt to Lott, as the show ended. Then, a couple of weeks later, Anthony Lake was on *Meet the Press*. The questioner was NBC's Tim Russert, who had served on the staffs of New York senator Daniel Patrick

Moynihan and New York governor Mario Cuomo before becoming the network's Washington bureau chief. Small world.
But upside down. The 1997 speaker at one of the country's
premier political platforms—the Al Smith Dinner, which is
sponsored by the Roman Catholic Archdiocese of New York
and is often a forum for presidents—was none other than
NBC's Tim Russert. Upside down again: Two months after
that, NBC News announced that Russert's old contract would
be extended until four years into the twenty-first century.
Talent, which he has, was not mentioned—only the fact that
Meet the Press was showing $25 million a year in net profit.

And then there was Susan Molinari, the perky Republican
congresswoman from New York who gave up her seat to join
CBS as a talk-show host, saying that all she ever wanted as a
kid was to be on television. Politics, it seems, was a means to
that end. As for the network, CBS News president Andrew
Heyward paid a high compliment to Molinari: "She repre-
sents the demographics we're trying to reach."

Back at the White House, I asked Tony Lake's successor as
national security adviser, Samuel (Sandy) Berger, a question
about the old days and the new. Who was more important
now in the making of United States foreign policy—Peter
Peterson, the Wall Street wise man and former Cabinet
officer serving as president of the Council on Foreign Relations in New York, or Thomas Friedman, the young *New York
Times* reporter who had recently returned from overseas assignments to write on diplomatic and economic affairs in
Washington?

"Who's Pete Peterson?" Berger said as a joke. The question
was ridiculous. The White House holds regular meetings

about what Friedman thinks or what he might do tomorrow. Some of the younger folk at those meetings have to be told who Peterson is—or was.

In the American journalism business, education traditionally came after fame, after power, and after better money. Usually it's the other way around. Focusing on Woodward and Bernstein, stories about them and about Watergate almost invariably mentioned that Bob Woodward graduated from Yale, because not many reporters did. Carl Bernstein was more typical; he had never finished college and had begun his career as a copyboy on the *Washington Star* and bounced around a couple of other papers before making it to the *Washington Post*.

As journalism became a more glamorous way to make a living, there was a steady banging at the doors of newspapers, magazines, and television stations by young men and women. There was also a boom in applicants to journalism schools around the country. From 1967 to 1986 the numbers of students earning bachelor's degrees in journalism increased sixfold.[12]

It is my sad duty here—sad and disloyal because I have taught journalism at Columbia, UCLA, and the University of Southern California—to report that many thousands of practitioners and instructors do not believe that journalism studies are worth four years of any student's life. How much does someone need to know about the subtleties of keystroking? The regard of practitioners with the power to hire journalism graduates may be demonstrated by the experience relayed to me by my students. Those engaging bright young folks have told me over the years that they have never been asked about their grades. Print bosses ask for "your clips": show me what you've written. Television types ask for "your tapes": show me what you can do on camera. I am partial to energetic students who learn history, literature, and economics— young people who can work like journalists without thinking like journalists. There is more to life than who said what today or yesterday.

That prejudice may have something to do with the fact that only one-fifth of those journalism graduates of the 1970s and 1980s found jobs at newspapers, with magazines, or in broadcasting; many were educated in departments of communications and aimed for higher-paying work in advertising or public relations. Remember that in the most beloved fictional representation of the tribe at work, *The Front Page,* written by Charles MacArthur and Ben Hecht in 1928, the reporter hero, Hildy Johnson, wants to go into the advertising business because he's getting married and the ad game pays more than Chicago newspapering.

Whatever else all those new degrees mean, they can be used to thin out the crowds of kids desperate to see their names in print or their faces on television. Personnel departments can cut the workload by saying they only interview graduates of journalism schools—or even that they will only interview those with graduate degrees. Newspaper jobs are hard enough to find these days, but television is even tougher. Surveys these days indicate that there are actual television news jobs for only one in ten J-school graduates.

The numbers of degree-credentialed applicants are new, but the low pay and high attitude in newsrooms are not. Newsroom old guards have generally thought you could learn all you needed to know in a week or so on the job. If a wannabe journalist really wanted to go to college, he was advised to spend those happy days reading history and economics—and any prose that floated like a butterfly and stung like a bee. A. J. Liebling, the great *New Yorker* press critic, had graduated from Columbia University's Graduate School of Journalism, Joseph Pulitzer's school. But this was Liebling's evaluation in later years: "It had all the intellectual status of a training program for future employees of the A&P."[13]

Times have changed more than attitudes. After forty years in network news, Av Westin, the vice-president of ABC News, complains, "The J-schools are turning out mechanics who can't write, even for television, and have no story sense." The complaint of many newspaper editors is that graduates think reporting is nothing more than using Lexis-Nexis, a computerized data base of news clippings and legal precedents. The service is sold cheaply at universities, but it is so expensive in the real world that few small newspapers or law firms can afford to use it.

The attitude at many journalism schools seems to be a cracked-mirror image of Liebling and Westin. Lana Rakow, director of the School of Communications at the University of North Dakota, has said this about her program and students: "Our students talk about information and technology, not journalism. We do not want to single out any particular field." In case you missed the message, she added: "Students will all be communicators."[14]

Of what? Scarlet fever? Apprehension?

However they got into the business, working journalists

(as opposed to owners and publishers) have generally been seen as political animals, usually as liberals pushing a hidden political agenda. A survey of journalists conducted by the University of Connecticut after the 1996 presidential election found that 91 percent of journalists based in Washington had voted for the more liberal of the candidates, President Clinton. I have been a part of the "Washington press corps," and that number seemed ridiculous to me. But others believed it, and their perception makes it real in a way. It does not matter whether polling is true or accurate. If people believe it or act on it, polling has a life and power of its own—it creates a baseline for decision making, or for not making decisions perceived to be unpopular.

That said, I would argue that the liberalism of the elite press is more cultural than political. The stars pretty much share the social attitudes of other well-educated and high-earning Americans, beginning with an aversion to progressive income taxes. A high-earner, Tim Russert again, made that point in May 1995 during one of two interesting shows put into Larry King's CNN time slot when the ask-master was on vacation.

Prominent political figures sat in for the host. Those politicians chose to turn the tables on important journalists. Here are excerpts from the shows, with former vice-president Dan Quayle, a Republican, and former Texas governor Ann Richards, a Democrat, questioning newsies. The group included Russert; Rita Braver, the White House correspondent of CBS News; syndicated columnist Charles Krauthammer; Dan Rather, the anchorman of CBS News; Cokie Roberts of ABC News; and Jane Pauley, host of NBC's *Dateline*.

Ann Richards: "Cokie, I know that there are institutions or foundations or think tanks in Washington that really don't represent any thinking, or very few people, across the country. And yet, you all quote statistics and stuff like that from them, like they were some legitimate organization."

Cokie Roberts: "The fact is that some of the kinds of people that establishment media wrote off as crackpots have become very powerful people. So you have to be careful in saying, 'Gee, those people don't count; therefore we don't pay any attention to them.' I think that what caused a lot of the upset about the media, in the sense that we were liberal and elite and out of touch and all those things, was the fact that we weren't paying enough attention to voices other than the ones that we knew well."

Dan Rather: "Some of those crackpots are now running the country."

Jane Pauley: "But those very 'crackpots' who then have come to power are keeping their eye on the media. My sense of change in the institution since I've been in it is that it is much more nervous about being accused of not being balanced."

When Quayle got his chance the next night, the former vice-president began: "Where is the balance? Is there liberal bias in the media? . . . Can we admit that there is?"

Rita Braver took the first crack at that, saying "the media" takes great pains to be fair.

"I'm not saying that it's not fair," said Quayle, "but it's fair through the liberal prism."

Then Russert said, "I think there's more of a cultural bias than a political bias."[15]

. . . . "The Tribe" . . . .

Like Rodney Dangerfield, many conservative commentators and thinkers don't get no respect from career journalists. They may be admired for their political impact, or envied for their corporate and foundation support and impressive book sales, but they are not respected or affirmed intellectually by the tribe or by the aging "liberal" cultural elite. No matter how smart or literate or successful they are, the new conservative intelligentsia—or counterintelligentsia—are seen by most of us as political activists, not political chroniclers or commentators. You can learn from them, but you can't trust them. At their best, which can be very good—particularly in books, in *Wall Street Journal* editorials, and in the asides of P. J. O'Rourke—the conservatives are occasionally cross with one another but generally stick to ideological duty, compiling and distributing only information that works for their side. They are pamphleteers, not essayists.

The scorned "liberals" can seem pathetic when they beat up on Bill Clinton or any other ideological companion who actually wins power. But that's the point: cultural respect and affirmation come from choosing argument over power—and so far, most of the new conservative commentators and intelligentsia seem incapable of biting the hands that feed them so well.

Political liberals, me among them, may have prisms, but they, the conservatives, seem to have bigger megaphones. Rush Limbaugh alone gets more electronic exposure than all the lefties on the continent. Anybody with a dollar can find out what William Safire or George Will (a former Republican congressional staffer) or the editorial writers of the *Wall Street Journal* think most every day of the year. The nonfiction best-seller list of the 1990s was generally dominated by provocative conservative authors. Even public television was projecting more and more faces of the Right—people like William F. Buckley and Peggy Noonan—pushing out the liberals who found a home there years ago. A "Christian conservative," Pat Robertson, has his own channel.

Conservatives, in obvious fact, have done a tremendous job in getting their ideas across in mainstream media—and getting more than a few bully pulpits for themselves. A lot of the credit for that should go to William E. Simon, the Wall Streeter who was secretary of the treasury under two Republican presidents. His 1978 book, a best-seller called *A Time for Truth,* ended with a strategy that worked: "I know of nothing more crucial than to come to the aid of the intellectuals and writers who are fighting on my side . . . A powerful counterintelligentsia can be organized to challenge our ruling [liberal] opinion makers . . . An audience awaits its [conservative] views."[16]

So it did. Simon urged corporate America to use its "public affairs" contributions to support intellectuals of the Right— in journalism, universities, and think tanks. To show the way, he used a foundation he controlled, the John M. Olin Foundation in Indianapolis, to create university chairs for such conservative thinkers as Irving Kristol and Allan Bloom. The Olin Foundation also played a part in the creation of rightwing newspapers on college campuses, beginning with the *Dartmouth Review.* Those little journals spread the conservative agenda, and, perhaps more important, recruited and trained a new generation of bright, edgy, conservative writers, scattered now at newspapers and magazines across the country.

It was an idea whose time had come. Yes, Cokie Roberts of ABC News is the daughter of two Democratic members of Congress—Hale Boggs, the late Majority Leader of the House, and his widow, Lindy Boggs. Columnist Mark Shields and CNN's Jeff Greenfield served Democratic officeholders, as did Russert. But on the other side of the journalistic equation, David Gergen, William Safire of the *New York Times,* television ringmaster John McLaughlin, Pat Buchanan of *Crossfire,* and Diane Sawyer of ABC are all among the most influential voices in the American press—and they have a secret or forgotten bond. They all served together in the White House, on the staff of that well-known liberal, Richard Nixon.

"Give Them What They Want!"

In the early 1930s Carl Ackerman, the dean of Columbia Journalism School, traveled the country interviewing "distinguished men and women," a group that included bankers, college presidents, governors, generals, clergymen—even two Nobel laureates. "What are the most important charges against the press by this interested and educated minority?" he began in a speech to the American Society of Newspaper Editors on April 29, 1933. In the reverse order that David Letterman would later make famous, Ackerman's answers read like this:

10. That the press cannot be an impartial and true advocate of public service so long as its owners are engaged or involved in other businesses.

9. That newspapers are interested primarily in day by day news developments and do not follow through to give the reader a continuous and complete account of what is happening.

8. That headlines frequently do not correctly reveal the facts and the tenor of the articles.

7. That the newspapers make heroes of criminals by their romantic accounts of gang activities.

6. That newspapers do not lead in public affairs, but follow the leadership of organized minorities.

5. That most reporters are inaccurate when reporting interviews.

4. That news values are often superficial and trivial.

3. That financial news is promotional rather than informative.

2. That the newspaper violates the individual right of privacy.

1. That newspaper standards are determined by circulation. That the press gives the public what it wants rather than what it needs.[1]

More than sixty years and a few new media later, this list and the questions journalism asks itself have not changed all that much. In 1997 the editor of the *Boca Raton News,* Wayne Ezell, said: "If readers said they wanted more comics and less foreign news, in a market driven economy, I'm going to give them more comics and less foreign news."[2] At the same time, NBC News anchorman Tom Brokaw was saying that his company was "breaking the mold" and would cut back on "dull" stories from Washington and foreign countries. Actually, he spoke after the fact: network television coverage of foreign stories, measured in minutes, dropped by almost two-thirds in just four years, from 1992 to 1996.

The argument over who decides what is "news"—journalists or customers—was joined across time by Susan Miller, a vice-president of Scripps-Howard, and William Shawn, the editor of the *New Yorker* magazine. She said: "Newspapers are to be of service to readers and are not staffed by a Brahmin class that was chosen to lecture the population. People who refuse to be service-oriented will leave in disgust and say we're pandering and will call us bad names—but they will leave." He had said almost twenty years earlier: "There is a fallacy in that calculation . . . The fallacy is if you edit that way, to give back to readers only what they think they want, you'll never give them something new they didn't know about. You stagnate . . . The whole thing begins to be circular. Creativity and originality and spontaneity goes out of it."[3]

Another difference between Miller and Shawn is this: she's alive and he's dead. And what used to be considered the news is failing. In March 1998, in preparation for a journalism conference at the Annenberg School for Communication at the University of Southern California, the Project for Excellence in Journalism and the Medill News Service issued a report called *Changing Definitions of News: A Look at the Mainstream Press over Twenty Years.* The group compared print and broadcast reports, 3,760 in all, for the month of March in 1977, 1987, and 1997. The news operations studied included the front pages of the *New York Times* and the *Los Angeles Times,* the three nightly network news programs, and the entire contents of *Time* and *Newsweek.* Some of the conclusions were:[4]

In 1977, more than half of all stories (52 percent) were basically straight news accounts of what had happened. By 1997 that figure had fallen to less than one in three stories (32 percent).

The number of stories about government dropped from one in three stories to one in five . . . The number of stories about foreign affairs dropped from nearly one in four to about one in every six . . . The number of stories about celebrity tripled, from one in every fifty stories to one out of every fourteen.

Time and *Newsweek* had the same cover as *People* magazine seven times as often in 1997 as in 1979 . . . In 1977, nearly one in five cover stories concerned policy or ideas. By 1987, that had fallen to just one in twenty covers, where it remains.

The greatest new shift in emphasis of network news was a marked rise in the number of stories about scandals, up from just one-half of one percent to 17 percent in 1987 and 15 percent in 1997.

Eleanor Clift of *Newsweek* and *The McLaughlin Group*—a reporter old enough to remember the way it was and young enough to be part of the way it is—said this: "You've got to interest people in a world that is very fast-paced. You've got to grab their attention, and often that is done through making news more entertaining."[5]

There is substantial guilt in the business about this. *Nightline,* Ted Koppel's ABC News program, is among the more serious and most distinguished of network news offerings, but it did cover the murder trial of O. J. Simpson and the death of England's Princess Diana as if life itself depended on the outcome of the sensations of the day. So in speaking at the 1997 dinner of the Committee to Protect Journalists, Koppel was both confessing and preaching when he said:

We are free to write and report whatever we think is important. But if what is important does not appeal to the reading or viewing appetites of our consumers, we'll give them something that does. No one is holding a gun to our heads. No one lies awake at night, dreading a knock on the door. We believe it to be sufficient excuse that "We are giving the public what it wants."

We react too much and anticipate too little. We struggle to be first with the obvious. The most important events of the last couple of years have not been the Simpson trial and the death of Princess Diana . . . We have more tools at our disposal and we are more skillful at applying them than any previous generation of journalists . . . We have the responsibility to do more: to focus on foreign events and to explain to the American public how and why those events have an impact on all of us. We need to help our viewers find their way through the blankets of fogs laid down by spin doctors, media advisers, and public affairs officers.

Perhaps we have too many tools. Advances in survey research techniques have created montages and mirages of numbers, lists, and ratings that cloud men's minds. Politicians, journalists, and entertainers are all in service to the gods of data that are telling them they know what people want. The warnings and wisdom of great men fade before the numbers. Give us data, data, data. Forget Albert Einstein. He once told a student, "Become a public opinion pollster. There you will never be unemployed. We know, after all, that people are ruled by being told tall stories—so the rulers must constantly test and see what they can get away with."[6]

These days, we are all constantly testing or being tested—a dubious luxury made possible by the new technologies. The biggest tester of all in recent years has been the forty-seventh president. When President Clinton returned to the White House after going to France for elaborately staged ceremonies commemorating the fiftieth anniversary of the 1944 D-Day landings in Normandy, the numbers had him banging his desk and shouting at no one in particular. What was he shouting about? "All that work and my approval went up just one-and-one-half points. Can you believe it?"[7]

Yes.

The president's dependence on survey research was such that the leader of Great Britain's Labour Party, Tony Blair, passed on this thought to British newsmen after a meeting in the White House: "I do remember something Clinton said, which is that there is no one more powerful in the world today than a member of a focus group. He said, 'If you really want to change things and if you want to get listened to, that's where you want to be.'"[8]

It was a joke, of course. I hope. But it has come close to that. The real shadow cabinets on both sides of the Atlantic are often a thousand or so randomly selected poll respondents, or even shifting groups of eight to twelve men and women paid to sit around a table responding to the questions and directions of a psychologist or pseudo-psychologist— with politicians and their spin doctors watching and listening on the other side of a one-way mirror. And journalism is doing exactly the same thing in its frantic efforts to find out what people are willing to spend fifty cents for—and to get it to them as fast as possible. News is being created by a journalism of artificial insemination.

Candidates, lobbyists, newspapers, magazines, and television news organizations each have their own numbers, including the "spin" numbers collected with misleading questions or rigged polling designed to influence Congress or the public. The Republican "Contract with America," announced before the 1994 congressional elections, was not a declaration of conservative dogma. It was a marketing plan constructed with poll numbers and focus groups. The killer argument for a balanced federal budget, repeated every day by the Speaker of the House, Newt Gingrich, was that 80 percent of Americans favor it. They may not understand it and 50 percent of them may think Elvis is alive, but the recitation of big numbers has a weight of its own.

That is why Gingrich went nuts on October 26, 1995, after reading the morning's *New York Times*. He called a press conference to rant about a Times/CBS Poll which reported two out of three respondents' saying that they preferred protecting Medicare when they were asked the following question (one of ninety-six in the poll): "If you had to choose, would you prefer balancing the federal budget or preventing Medicare from being significantly cut?"

Said Speaker Gingrich, "This poll is a disgraceful example of disinformation. What we get are deliberately rigged questions that are totally phony."[9]

Whoa! Maybe silly or ephemeral, but "totally phony"? The reason Gingrich flipped tells something about poll-driven politics. Republicans had been pushing for balanced-budget legislation by chanting "80 percent." He had to try to destroy new numbers that displaced his own. So he had to say the "liberal media" were lying.

Which numbers were right? Perhaps none. But that doesn't matter. They are spoken and printed, therefore they are—the numbers are created events—until they are superseded by new numbers. They substitute for thinking. "A lot of the coverage is poll-driven," said CBS's Dan Rather. "That is one big change."[10]

It is not only CBS News. Numbers tend to sweep away editors, reporters, and, sometimes, common sense and what used to be called judgment. The seductive hint of science and certainty relieves decision makers of responsibility; if things go wrong, the blame can be laid on the numbers. The statistical alchemy can be used to minimize human error—and humans, too. *Time* magazine and CNN combined efforts during the 1996 presidential campaign to create something called "Election Monitor," continuous polling of a fixed sample of five thousand voters. Every little movement had a meaning all its own. "It'll give us a moving picture of voter opinion," said Stephen Koepp, *Time*'s overseer of polling. His counterpart at CNN, Tom Hannon, added: "We're going to use these surveys as the foundation of a lot of our reporting."[11]

On May 27, 1993, out on the White House lawn, one of Rather's colleagues, Harry Smith of CBS's *This Morning* show, was working an audience of a couple of hundred tourists. Rattling off a series of poll numbers, Smith, who is paid more than one million dollars a year for doing such things, turned to President Clinton and said:

"I know you don't pay attention to this sort of stuff—polls. You never pay attention probably, right?"

The comedy over, Smith turned to the crowd, spouted a few more numbers, and said:

"The negatives are now higher than the positives in the polls . . . There's a feeling in the country and I think the people here reflect it. I think people in America want you to succeed, but I just want a raise of hands this morning—and don't be intimidated just because you're in the Rose Garden—do you feel like he could be doing a better job? Raise your hands if you think so. Don't be intimidated. Don't be intimidated. There's a lot of folks who feel that way. Do you feel like there's a gap between the promises of the campaign and the performance thus far? If you think so, raise your hands. A lot of folks feel that way. What went wrong?"[12]

What went wrong, indeed. Inside the White House, Sandy Berger, the national security adviser, answered that question: "Machines can't think, but they change the way people do."[13]

Polls have advanced from being the crutches holding up cautious politicians and journalists to becoming the national superstructure of public opinion democracy—almost everything else hangs from them. Otherwise sensible editors and candidates collapse in the face of "scientific" numbers. But the only thing scientific about polls is probability theory. The theory, provable within a discrete margin of error, is that in a universe of black and white beans, the ratio of black to white in, say, 1,500 beans selected at random will be the same as the ratio in all the millions of beans in that universe, plus or minus the predictable margin of error.

From there on, it's only make believe, because neither questions, nor questioners, nor respondents are as inert as beans. But, again, it does not matter whether polls are right or wrong; it only matters that decision makers use them as if they were correct and true. Peter Hart, one of the president's pollsters, added this early in Bill Clinton's tenure: "Clinton is a president who doesn't need new information or more information. He explores it all . . . and the effects are dramatic, short-term impulses, which means a constantly changing course."[14]

Such things, and the collusion of the press, are at the heart of a revolution—a technological one—blowing through and away many of the checks and balances that were supposed to slow down the governing of the United States. Polls and more polls, private, public, and continuous, have replaced ideas, ideology, and passion in American politics. In American journalism, the questions and numbers are stories without reporters. "GIGO" ("Garbage In, Garbage Out") was an early warning that seems to have been forgotten in our reverence for computers and everything that can be plugged into them.

Peter Hart added this: "The world of public opinion has come into great collision with the art of governance. In the old Washington, there were two or three polls, principally Gallup and Harris, and each one took a couple of weeks to do, going door-to-door . . . Now, with new kinds of telephones and computers for tabulation, in a half-hour you can come back and say, 'This is what the public thinks.'"

You can also say: this is what the public wants—and the way they want it.

They want it short. So give them what they want. Better, just give them a list. Lists, in fact, are perfect condensed news in a country with all the symptoms of Attention Deficit Disorder. There is more information around than we can process, and lists, like polls, cut to the chase.

This is our new shorthand: The top ten . . . the best one hundred . . . the Fortune 500 . . . the Forbes 400 . . . the best colleges . . . the best cities to live in . . . the best hospitals . . . of the year . . . of the month . . . of the week . . . of the day . . . up to the minute. I came across the two-page "executive biography" of a Texas entrepreneur named Kenny Troutt (number 105 on *Forbes* magazine's list of richest Americans) which includes a half-page of Troutt listings, including 478th in Net Profits in the Fortune 500, seventy-second in *Inc.* magazine's 500 (fastest-growing companies), second in the *Dallas Business Journal's* Fast Tech 50, and first in the CEO Institute's Top Hundred.

The lists may or may not be a good thing—other choices are often dangerous little bits of information or absolute ignorance—but they fit the times. The same thing is true of starred movie reviews (or Siskel and Ebert's thumbs) and of the numerous numerical ratings of cars, wines, and money managers.

And then there is the continuous polling that produces the television ratings. I was trashing a television program one day with Norman Lear, one of the most successful producers in the history of the medium. He cut me off and with uncharacteristic anger said, "You know what ruined television? When your newspaper, the *New York Times,* began publishing the Nielsen ratings. That list every week became all anyone cared about."

Those, in fact, were what we now call the good old days. Now the *Times* runs a dozen lists every Monday ranking movies, television shows, and computer programs according to how much they grossed the week before. Of course, the paper of record always had a best-seller list for books. Once it was for readers; now it is a decision-making device for the country's largest booksellers, who try to pull in customers by discounting listed books.

"Those lists are one gigantic pain in the ass," said David Komansky, chairman of Merrill-Lynch. "It's more social than financial, but it affects decision making. Ted Turner was right when he said that there are people on the *Forbes* list who will not give to charity or anything else because giving might drop them lower on the list—or even drop them off."[15]

A few years ago, an academic researcher named Francis Fukuyama received a good deal of attention by proclaiming in print and speech "the End of History." He overreached, but still he may have been on to something. Perhaps what we are seeing is the End of News—at least as we have known it. People are just getting out of the way. There are words that make eyes glaze over, or make fingers twitch reflexively on the television remote. Does anyone not personally involved, or not making money on information transfers, pay any attention past the word "Bosnia"? Or past "Rwanda"? "Burundi"? "Zaire"? "Taliban"? "Hubbell"? "Greenspan"? "McVeigh"?

The electronic storytellers have figured this out already. Each night now, network newscasts seem to come closer to presenting evening news without news. Pictures, yes, as well as inspiration, self-help, medical advice, consumer outrage— and blood and fire. Years ago, when Communist authorities controlled television in the old Soviet Union, the evening news in Moscow was the same every day. First, an official somewhere was handing a bouquet to a worker who had exceeded her factory's quota for tractor gear-shifts. Then came *The West in Flames!*—a montage of film pirated from satellite transmissions in Western Europe and the United States, depicting explosions, chain collisions, crime, and other sorts of mayhem. Now the Soviet Union is no more, and American networks and local stations are showing the

West in flames every day. Forget what used to be called "tell stories."

The video product, say the numbers, is pretty much what people want—or rather, they are not getting what they don't want. More and more, I think viewers and readers do not want complicated and emotionally complex stories that remind them of their own frustrations. Real news reflects the speeded up and piled on changes of modern life—and you don't get that on *Entertainment Tonight* or *Hard Copy* and other pseudo-news shows.

This did not happen overnight. In 1978, ABC News's Av Westin was asked to see if he could do something to save a prime-time nonfiction show called *20/20*. It was scheduled to be canceled in six weeks, but by then Westin had it humming along and the ratings got better and better. I asked Westin how he had done it, and he said he began at the ABC research department, asking what people wanted on prime-time television.

"I got a one-word answer," he said. "The word was 'entertainment.'

"So I put on the Rock Star of the Week. We continued the same kind of human-interest stories we had been running about people's troubles and triumphs, but I made sure the people were celebrities—rock stars and movie stars."[16]

It worked. As we talked, the show was in its twentieth year. It was a success. But was it news? Oh, the irony, the inevitability of it all. Television is an entertainment medium; it has always been unsure in packaging and delivering news.

Newspapers, on the other hand, have always been clunky when trying to entertain. Influenced by polls and focus groups, newspapers and local television news operations stumbled into an entertainment trap. Trying to expand or hold their audiences, many daily journals went from being a local necessity, essential to community life, to becoming just another entertainment, not a very good one, competing for public attention and focus group approval.

News as Entertainment

So Av Westin saved *20/20* by figuring out how to make squishy-soft news look like entertainment. Then he moved on to tabloid television for a while, running *Inside Edition,* one of the first syndicated pseudo-news shows. Jim Bellows, former editor of the *New York Herald Tribune* and a couple of other major newspapers, moved on, too, becoming a multimedia role model by bringing his significant journalistic expertise to television (*Entertainment Tonight,* or *ET*) and the Internet (*Excite*). He saved *ET,* another of the syndicated entertainment "news" shows, by teaching the folks there how to make movie studio promotion look like news—with anchors, commentary, and "reporters" sticking microphones in pretty faces and asking tame little preapproved questions.

Real news can barely compete with the sort that's on television. The question now is whether real news or hard news can survive at the networks. Ed Fouhy, whose three-network career somewhat paralleled Westin's at ABC News, says this now: "When you're the executive producer of a network prime-time show, you become keenly aware of how intense

the market pressures are . . . You're competing against entertainment shows, and you've got to have numbers in the same
league or you're judged a failure . . . You start to pull your
punches."[1]

Such men created a demi-news different from real news in
the most fundamental way: *20/20, Entertainment Tonight,
Dateline,* and their many imitators make you feel good. The
Disney Company went a great leap farther in 1994—before it
bought ABC and ABC News—by creating a syndicated television show called *Movie News,* a collage of news-like segments
on the making of its own films.

Real news is another business, even if some of it, too, is
owned by Disney. News often makes you mad as hell and
depressed about your own individual powerlessness. The
entertainment-as-news and news-as-entertainment shows
emerged and merged years after Marshall McLuhan wrote
that the medium was the message. Popular news modified
one of his most interesting insights. People who complained
that the evening news was all "bad news," he said, did not
understand what they were seeing. The "good news" was the
commercials. Buy this or try that and you get the job, get the
money, and get the girl—all endings are happy, or at least
pleasurable.

One of the most telling McLuhan predictions was that
sports would replace politics on television. And so it has, in
the most dramatic displacement of news by entertainment.
The first shared American experience in television's beginnings were the week-long Republican and Democratic national conventions to choose presidential candidates. Those
spectacles have been superseded now by Super Bowls, Final

Fours, and such. On television, Michael Jordan, Tiger Woods, and other heroes of the weekend are more interesting than presidents or writers. That includes political writers, who have been trying to make elections a sport—"the horse race"—in a touching attempt to keep television's attention.

Joel Connable, a senior at the University of Southern California who worked on preparations for the conference mentioned in the previous chapter, offered a quick synopsis of his dealings with local television news executives and correspondents in Los Angeles: "After a while I realized that they use 'interesting' and 'entertaining' as synonyms."

The business of television, to say the least, has evolved. It has become our environment, more like weather than a medium. In a mobile society, the people on television are our real neighbors, the people we gossip about—so much so that the death of Princess Diana or the murder of Bill Cosby's son or Bill Clinton's indiscretions hit millions upon millions of people with the force of a tragedy in the family. When political conventions no longer served television's purposes, the greatest democracy in the world changed its nominating system. The conventions were effectively replaced by primary elections—with the Iowa caucuses or New Hampshire primary becoming the first ballot. Perfect for television, the primaries are simple and straightforward, lists and numbers compiled in a single day—and the polls don't close until after the big commercial hours of prime time. The same kind of television-driven rule changes have occurred in sports, as anyone who has actually gone to a National Football League game can tell you. During longer and longer commercial breaks, players aimlessly wander around the field waiting for the television people to signal that they can resume play. And of course the "two-minute warning" is not an alarm but a rigidly scheduled final commercial break before half-time and the end of the game.

Programming a network is something like sculpture: what you take off is as important as what you put on. After Jane Pauley left NBC's *Today*, someone asked her what had changed over her thirteen years. She answered: "We used to do poetry readings on the *Today* show—a lot of that, and string quartets."[2] No more, not even on public television.

Competing with television has changed or is changing, too. Venerable magazines and newspapers folded during the television years, but the news on the networks and local stations could be seen as an animated extension of print journalism, largely because people like Ed Fouhy and Walter Cronkite began their careers in the newspaper business. Again, no more. J. Randolph Murray, the editor of the *Anniston Star*, said: "The news and information that has been delivered on radio and television over the past couple of decades has gone through the same newspaper editing process. In the last few years, though, the explosion of talk radio is delivering raw half-facts, half-truths, and isolated facts to a wide audience."[3]

The *new* radio and television people are just that—a *new* breed. The drive to entertain is liberating for them. A television producer named Alan Landsberg, who had covered the White House before switching over to entertainment television, once told me: "I used to stand out there at the gate looking at the building and trying to figure out what they were doing inside. Now I can just make it up."

Actually, now nonfiction television makes it up, too. NBC's coverage of the 1996 Summer Olympics in Atlanta must have been the end of innocence for many viewers. It's only sports, but . . . It turned out that NBC Sports confidently led viewers out of real time into a digitally edited world where what was happening next had already happened. In that virtual reality, events began when NBC wanted them to, stopped for commercials and profiles of athletes that seemed uncannily prescient about who would win and why. Like children, millions of us sat up late into the night watching the dramatic bravery of American gymnasts defeating the world—without being told all this had happened hours before NBC allowed us to look into the virtual world they had created to entertain us.

I should have known. Remember, this is entertainment. Networks pay to cover the spectacle. Television sports contracts allow the networks to exploit but not expose. Every once in a while, you see the disconnection with real journalism. Watching the Philadelphia Eagles of the National Football League play one night late in 1997, on television, I saw a sideline scene of the quarterback, Ty Detmer, and a running back, Ricky Watters, pushing each other around. "What was that about?" asked one of the announcers after the game ended. His man on the field said he didn't know, because "we've been told that we shouldn't talk to the players about that."

Back in Atlanta at the Olympics, it was not athletes but nature and time that were being manipulated. It was close to midnight as I sat at home in New York and the television sky in Georgia was changing from dark to light and back again—a small technical difficulty yet to be worked out. But it will be one day—or night. "Lighting, on number six, bring that sky down . . . That's it—darker, darker, good, good. Now give us some rain, just a little."

This is why control rooms are called control rooms. Don't "Get real!"—get virtual. Don't "Get a life!"—NBC has one for you. And everything we see now will be shown forever on nostalgia channels, so we can all escape forever, stay forever young together in a retrievable past of old movies and ball games. Digital imaging and things similarly named are going to change all information—or, more precisely, all reality. News is the "reality" I happen to care about, and, like most people losing a grip on change, I would kind of prefer things to stay the way they were. But that is not going to happen. Never has. For fun or profit or political advantage, there will soon enough be a scandal in which someone uses the techniques that put actor Tom Hanks in conversation with John F. Kennedy in an electronically altered 1962 film clip for the movie *Forrest Gump*.

Technology is defeating time. All things human can happen at the same time—as long as there be film or tape or digits. Forget about "Seeing is believing." But hang onto "Believe nothing you hear and only half of what you see."

Yes, but which half?

In a 1997 multimedia irony, a television commercial made for the American Newspaper Publishers Association, urging people to read newspapers, showed retired general Norman Schwarzkopf sitting in front of a Rocky Mountain vista with a bird flying across the beautiful scene. The bird was a phony—hatched from a computer, not an egg. The commercial's producer, advertising man Jerry Della Femina, thought the original mountain shot, which was real, looked too perfect. So to make it look more real than the real thing, he created the bird. If he'd felt like it, he could have photographed a real bird and put in a phony Schwarzkopf.[4]

The final irony in this little morality play is that in 1991, the real General Schwarzkopf systematically and effectively did whatever it took to prevent real press coverage of the Gulf War. He acted in a great military tradition. In 1864 General William Tecumseh Sherman, who led the brutal Union march through Georgia, ordered the execution of a reporter whose dispatches he considered helpful to the Confederate enemy; he called off the firing squad only on the direct orders of President Lincoln. Later he heard a rumor (false) that three correspondents had been killed in action, and said: "That's good. We'll have dispatches now from hell before breakfast."

My most memorable encounter with the military in information action was in 1984, during the United States–financed "secret" Contra war in Nicaragua. I ran into a blockade along a road in Honduras, near the Nicaraguan border. As I stepped out of my car, two C-47s swept over a mountain range near the Nicaraguan border and filled the sky with dozens of blossoming parachutes dropping armed men onto the ground several hundred yards distant. "What's with the paratroopers?" I asked the American officer standing next to me. He answered: "What paratroopers?"

The new technologies are blending generals, birds, presidents, fact, and fiction without warning to make movies and commercials. Humans are an adaptable breed and, in the long run, will work all this out by creating a mind picture of the world that serves their purposes. In the short run, though, you can see a startling confusion of realms. One example: If you are a parent, you are probably aware that there is a frightening amount of drinking and sexual violence on college campuses these days—and not much of it is making the news. If you talk to students about this, they become defensive and say that we, the ancients, had our fun and now want to cut off theirs. After listening to kids for a while, including your own, you realize that their picture of our youth comes from a movie, *Animal House.*

One of the stars of prime-time "reality programming," Jane Pauley of NBC's *Dateline,* has talked of a smaller but more deliberate confusion. "I'm always surprised," she said, "if I'm home watching television, and it's on NBC, and there's a promo for *Dateline,* and something I've done is promoted to entice America to watch . . . with this breathless, urgent voice using adjectives that I personally wouldn't have used, like 'shocked.' Everything is shocking . . . The promotion factor, which is very critical in prime time, does give you the wrong impression."[5]

Celebrities are the fuel of prime-time demi-news, as Av Westin learned, and America is extremely good at pumping them out of the ground. I found out just how good when my wife and I were living abroad, in Paris, in the mid-1980s. Coming home to New York periodically, we would fade conversationally when friends casually mentioned names we had never heard—new celebrities. We solved our cultural problems by subscribing to *People* magazine and soon were able to pretend we knew what was coming out of America's celebrity wells.

This is not new, although the speed and volume of it all have greatly lowered the threshold of fame. Celebrities have always been with us—medieval saints, for instance—and their notoriety has always been bankable, if not always fun, for all involved.

"It is impossible for us to subject the life of our second son to the publicity we feel was in large measure responsible for the death of our first child . . . I am appealing to the press to permit our children to lead lives of normal Americans."[6]

This was part of the statement Charles Lindbergh made when he announced in 1935 that he and his family were leaving the United States to try to escape the American press, particularly the New York tabloids. The papers of the day had lionized him after his startling solo flight from New York to Paris in 1927, and then hounded him after the kidnapping and murder of his first son in New Jersey in 1932.

The young hero said this of his marriage to Anne Morrow and their honeymoon trip: "For eight straight hours they circled about our boat, at anchor in a New England harbor . . . Occasionally they called across the water that if we posed for one picture they would go away."

As a matter of principle, Lindbergh refused to pose. Then he discovered that a New York reporter had bribed a servant, giving the man $2,000 to "betray the secrets of our house."

The great press critic of the day, George Seldes, wrote this of Lucky Lindy: "When he married privately, the tabloid press felt itself insulted. When he tried to take his honeymoon without benefit of publicity, the sensational press hounded him. One tabloid called him a 'Grade A celebrity,' therefore a public commodity, like gas or electric light."

Other "celebrities" joined in attacks on the press as reporters surrounded Lindy. Sinclair Lewis said, "Lindbergh cannot become engaged without 110,000,000 people leeringly looking on . . . For this is perhaps our greatest achievement over Europe; not our electric irons nor our concrete skyscraper constructions, but our changing of the ancient right of privacy so that most secret and perhaps agonized words of any human being are now the property of any swine who cares to read them."[7]

And almost all of this happened before nonfiction was bought out by fiction purveyors and the biggest of big business, corporations that operate on financial levels far above the small potato fields of the press. CBS News, along with fourteen television stations and thirty-nine radio stations, is part of Westinghouse. NBC News is part of General Electric, which also controls nine television stations, a radio network, and parts of ten cable networks. ABC News is a tiny part of the Disney entertainment empire, including dozens of newspapers and magazines, and television stations and cable systems reaching half the American people all day, all night. The Cable News Network, the feisty independent, is now part of Time-Warner, with a vast stable of magazines, cable channels, and book publishers. Not to be outdone, the News Corporation, the Australian corporate base of Rupert Murdoch's empire, has Fox News to go along with his newspapers, magazines, and satellites.[8]

"Network news shows have become arms of the entertainment business, making deals with movie publicists, letting them dictate how much time and how many appearances their clients will get," says Don Hewitt, the creator of CBS

News's *60 Minutes*. "When broadcasters ran the show, they said to news divisions, 'Make us proud.' The new owners say, 'Make us money.'"[9]

It is said that journalism and its little shop are disliked and distrusted by the public. Perhaps, but the owners have not had the confidence to rename their shows the *Westinghouse Evening News,* the *GE Nightly News,* or *Disney World News.* Not yet. Stay tuned—we'll be back after this message.

What's the Story?

"The question, 'What's the story?' remarkably concentrates the mind. It is where journalism begins."

This is from *Winds of Change,* by Betty Medsger, a 1996 report on journalism education published by the Freedom Forum, a foundation established by Frank Gannett, the founder of what would become the country's largest chain of newspapers. He had just become a part owner of his first paper, the *Gazette* in Elmira, New York, in the early 1900s, when a play called *The Stolen Story,* by Jesse Lynch Williams, opened in New York. In his 1911 *Collier's* series, Will Irwin used a scene from the play, written in a politically incorrect era, to illustrate what he called "the mysterious news sense":

(Enter Very Young Reporter; comes down to city desk with air of excitement.)

Very Young Reporter: Big story. Three dagoes killed by that boiler explosion.

The City Editor (Reading copy. Doesn't look up): Ten lines.

Very Young Reporter (Looks surprised and hurt. Crosses

over toward reporters' table. Then turns back to city desk.
Casual conversational tone): By the way. Funny thing.
There was a baby in a baby carriage within fifty feet of the
explosion, but it wasn't upset.

The City Editor (Looks up with professional interest): That's
worth a dozen dead dagoes. Write a half column.

(Very Young Reporter looks still more surprised, perplexed.
Suddenly the idea dawns on him. He crosses over to table,
sits down, writes.)

Commented Irwin: "Both saw news; but the editor went
further than the reporter. Italians killed by a boiler explosion
are so common as to approach the commonplace; but a freak
explosive chemistry which annihilates a strong man and does
not disturb a baby departs from it widely."

There you have it. That's what we do. That's why Michael
Bloomberg of Bloomberg Business News, suddenly one of the
world's largest employers of journalists, says it's not rocket
science. (Rocketry, actually, is not that complicated either—
just stuffing explosives in tin cans. Targeting and guidance—
that's tough.)

Were it a person, journalism would be diagnosed as depressed. The business has had ups and downs in the century
since the Very Young Reporter wrote his first big story.
Changes in technology and ownership, declining public interest, low morale among reporters losing faith in their own
journals and broadcasts, and impaired public trust seem to
have put the press on the wrong side of history, at least for
the moment. One of the most distinguished practitioners of
my generation, James D. Squires, editor of the *Chicago Trib-*

une for eight years, wrote this a few years after he'd resigned at the peak of his powers in 1989:

> For all its imperfections, the "press" traditionally has been a people-oriented, privately owned, public-spirited, politically involved enterprise concerned primarily with the preservation of democracy. That in itself was a major reason it survived in basically the same form for 200 years. But the press has lost that distinctive character, which means that it now has no better chance of survival than any other business, nor should it have. Under the new order, this news medium is no longer an institution dedicated to the public interest but rather a business run solely in the interest of the highest possible level of profitability.[1]

That's why Squires quit—and so did Kovach in Atlanta, Naughton in Philadelphia, and Tom White in Lincoln. But Squires was the most profoundly pessimistic of all, saying: "In the end, it may well be that the values and traditions of the free press will have to find refuge and nourishment in that other 'public sector' of our economy—the world of non-profit foundations and educational institutions. It may be here, and here alone, that public service journalism can survive—at least in some ivory tower—so it can eventually take root in the new world of electronic information delivery."

Ah, we could become monks rather than blacksmiths or bank tellers. Quill pens at the ready, we could make copies of the sacred texts. We could create a Diogenes Foundation.

C'mon. It's not that bad. But this is obviously the time to sound the alarm, to gain enough attention and create enough excitement (or controversy) to force a more public and more urgent debate about the role (or the survival) of what we called journalism. I, for one, welcomed the hypertense 1998 coverage and uncoverage of press decision making during the legal/political struggle between President Clinton and an independent prosecutor, Kenneth Starr—and, too, the public soul-searching after the revelation that writers for such respected journals as the *New Republic* and the *Boston Globe* had been making up entertaining stories and interesting quotes.

The questions are very hard for all of us who believe in what we do—and think there is a real chance that what we have learned and practiced could get lost in this spectacular technological shuffle. The lost tribe of America. We do, most of us, consider ourselves seekers of daily truth in a place and time where facts seem ever debatable. And we are frightened that journalism is not reproducing itself.

Old Farts who care can get discouraged looking at the new competition. I was gathering news before Jerry Yang of *Yahoo!* was born, but his Internet browser can take you most anywhere newspapers can—for free. I walked with him through his company's headquarters in Santa Clara, California, peeking at offices that looked like an industrial-strength version of my kids' rooms. In cubicles decorated with pizza boxes and sneakers and their aromas, young men and women were doing what reporters do—systematically gathering, ordering, and analyzing information for mass distribution.

"We didn't know what this was worth when we started," Yang said. "We just liked doing it, it was like watching TV . . . Luckily, greedy people were thinking for us. Everyone was using it because it was free. We started to charge the people who we were listing. They were just grad students like us, but we were collecting eyeballs and became a medium that could sell advertising."

So two grad students having fun can be a medium now. My competitors. Or are they? When we stopped for coffee, Yang said: "How do I learn about journalism?"

"Why do you want to do that?" I asked.

"We just had some trouble. On one of our pages we listed a link with a website called 'Jews for Jesus.' All hell broke loose with Jewish organizations. We had no idea what was going on. Would you have known?"

"Yes. Any reporter would."

"Even a Very Young Reporter," I thought. I guess that means we're going to be around awhile. What do people need from us? Or, what do they need us for? We will probably continue to have a monopoly on any news more complicated and serious than the stories listed as the top five of 1994 by the Associated Press: O. J. Simpson charged with murder; elections; baseball and hockey labor troubles; Susan Smith drowns her children; and Nancy Kerrigan and Tonya Harding on ice. Among the stories that did not make the list were the election of Nelson Mandela as president of a desegregated South Africa, or the genocidal war in Rwanda, or what you are paying in local taxes and why. Suburban lifestyle hints may be relaxing to read, if you have the time, but it's hard to believe that people will buy a paper or turn on the news for such discretionary fare.

What then is necessary? "Real news"? I used the phrase once in one of my classes at the University of Southern California, and a student asked, "What's that?" Good question.

My answer was: "The news you and I need to keep our freedom"—accurate and timely information on laws and wars, police and politicians, taxes and toxics. I listened once to a speaker from France describing the sophisticated and unwritten rules that shielded the private lives of France's public figures, and informal censorship of other news which might diminish the respect of citizens for those leaders or for France itself. Yes, I thought, and they lost their country. The press would not report that the emperor had no clothes and that his men were lying about the true state of French military defenses. In 1940 the Germans came and took France from the complacent and uninformed French.

Patrick Henry, who helped found the United States, put it this way more than two hundred years ago: "The press must prevent officials from covering with the veil of secrecy the common routine of business, for the liberties of the people never were, or never will be, secure when the transactions of their rulers may be concealed from them."[2]

"The higher function," wrote Will Irwin, "is to guard popular rights." And this might be the right time to clean up our act, get back on top of the old Fourth Estate role. Let government be government. And let the press be the press, with a little less polling and "Gotcha!" and a little more judgment and perspective. Of course, these faults are not new. My muse of the moment, Irwin, wrote in 1911: "There is a kind of muckraking, much in vogue of late, which consists in massing all the invidious facts about a man or an institution, and, by ignoring the sense of proportion, proving what appears to be a black case. Such work is accurate but not truthful."

Romantic as ever, he added: "The newspaper should be a gentleman—such is the whole formula. However, some arbiter of manners has said: 'It is never gentlemanly to knock a man down, but sometimes a gentleman must do it nevertheless.'"

Irwin even offered a code of ethics for gentlemen of the press:

First—Never, without special permission, print information which you learn at your friend's house or in your club. In short, draw a strict line between your social and professional life.

Second—Except in the case of criminals, publish nothing without the full permission of your informant. The caution, "But this is not for publication," stands between every experienced reporter and a world of live, sensational matter . . . It is not a question so much of morals as of convenience. In news-gathering, acquaintance is half the battle.

Third—Never sail under false colors. State who you are, what newspaper you represent, and whether or not your informant is talking for publication. If there is keyhole work to be done, leave that to the detectives, who work inside the law.

Fourth—Keep this side of the home boundary. Remember that when the suicide lies dead in the chamber there are wretched hearts in the hall, that when the son is newly in jail intrusion is torment to the mother.[3]

"Nearly all reporters who expect to stay in the business respect articles one and two," Irwin concluded. "Articles three and four, most of them would like to respect. They cannot do so, however, without permission of their directing editors or publisher, a court of last resort."

Nice! We would say: Keep your word; protect your sources. Common decency; common sense.

But sense and decency are sometimes the first casualties of the press in heat. The chase takes over in frenzies of speed and competition. That happened when the hounds were loosed on the White House in the second week of 1998. On January 17, *Newsweek,* which had been sniffing around rumors of presidential sex in the Oval Office, made a decision to postpone publishing a long story focusing on President Clinton and a young White House intern. *Newsweek*'s editors decided to hold off for a week, to look for more verification. Old-fashioned common sense.

Of course, not everyone liked the decision, beginning with Michael Isikoff, the reporter who had done most of the investigating. Things like that have happened to most of us, and the usual reaction is grumbling into a glass or two and then getting up to get answers to editors' doubting questions. Wait till next week! This time, though, someone from *Newsweek,* leaking with the same sense of purpose as government officials, called an Internet gossip columnist named Matt Drudge. In minutes and without the niceties of fact checking, Drudge was on-line, claiming a "World Exclusive!" All journalistic hell broke lose. Historical hell. Almost instantly the nation was wading through minute-to-minute multimedia reportage of rumors, affidavits, oaths, depositions—sex, lies, and audiotapes—more or less officially merging Old Fart journalism and Internet technology.

Hacks and hackers came together, dumping information as raw as sewage on the American people—who, it should be noted, seemed to be lapping up every tidbit. Drudge reported what he heard, on his own *Drudge Report* website, under the exuberant warning "Contains Graphic Description." *Newsweek,* which would not get another shot at graphic description for six days, put a 5,000-word story on its own website, claiming credit for the scoop it had not published, at least on paper. Within days, such estimable old-fashioned publications as the *Wall Street Journal* and the *Dallas Morning News* were also putting their stories-in-progress on the Internet, unwilling to wait the few hours until readers could see and touch their next editions—and before editors and reporters could check out new rumors and invisible sources.

Newsweek and the *Journal* lost control; they were pumping out immediate, plausible, and under-checked information. Great institutions, it seems, can spend decades developing systems and tests to weigh and evaluate information before publishing it in the old way—and then throw away those tests and restraints in the heat of the very old American struggle between native puritanism and the national tolerance essential to democracy. Even as they beat up on Drudge as a pseudo-journalistic bottom-feeder, *Newsweek* editors joined him, appearing across networks and 'Net to brag about what they had *almost* done. They were doing exactly the opposite of what they used to do in the old days—days that came to an end on that Saturday night, January 17— which was keep their mouths shut until their product hit the streets.

To make news matters worse, the television networks' three wise men, Dan Rather, Tom Brokaw, and Peter Jennings—who were all in Havana to cover a truly great story, the visit of a pope to godless communism in Cuba—abandoned their flocks of researchers and technicians to follow yonder star back to New York and Washington, and preach sonorously of the public policy aspects of oral sex.

It seemed the emperor actually had no clothes. And neither did we. One amazed observer, Bill Kovach, the former editor of the Atlanta newspapers, realized that he was watching a complete role-reversal between journalism and its public. Once upon a time, reporters and editors had been the national skeptics, sifting and evaluating news for readers and viewers; now, using the new technologies, the press was dumping information out by the ton and the readers and viewers were left to do the sifting, to sort it out for themselves.

Assuming 10 percent of it was true, or 95 percent of it was true, the question of which 10 percent or which 95 percent was generally left to the imagination. Much of the established press just abdicated responsibility and picked up speed—trying to catch up with electronic gossips and the spin masters of politics. The speed itself was great—and journalism will probably make better use of it in the digital future—but this time there was no captain to steer. Ben Bradlee, editor of the *Washington Post* in its most exciting Watergate days, said in the mid-1970s that his paper and staff were producing "a rough first draft of history." If that is true, the first speeded-up journalism produced in early 1998 by the union of news and the Internet was, at its best, the rough first draft of the first draft. Some of it was as rough or as marginal as reporters' notebooks—before scribbles were checked out to see whether they were true or important.

That is a tricky step beyond. All news organizations, including weeklies and monthlies, are going to have to be prepared to publish or broadcast or just announce twenty-four hours a day. There will be the excitement of the old-fashioned "Extra! Extra! Read all about it!" Deadlines focus the mind wonderfully, and it is possible that this newest kind of journalism will reinvigorate a tribe growing old. The interactivity of the Internet could also allow local papers and broadcasters to bring their readers and viewers into "newsrooms"—as in "chatrooms"—making them part of the process of gathering the news of the day.

That would help. The public's first reaction to the spectacle of 1998 was to blame the national embarrassment on the press. Our credibility ratings dropped far below even those of the emperor whose naked public and private behavior we had been mocking. Imagine that. Years of reporters' chipping away, and of politicians' general foolishness, had reduced the words "press" and "politician" almost to curses. Even dictionaries abandoned neutrality.

Defining "politician," Webster's Unabridged quickly slides from bland objectivity to high dudgeon: "1. A person who is active in party politics. 2. A seeker or holder of public office, who is more concerned about winning favor or retaining power than about maintaining principles . . . 6. A person who seeks to gain power or advancement within an organization in ways that are generally disapproved."

In May 1995 the governor of Texas, Ann Richards, caught that, or us, quite nicely in her one-show career as Larry King's replacement on CNN, turning to Dan Rather and asking: "Dan, a news story might say the White House influ-

enced, or tried to influence, the Housing Department, or the
Transportation Department. So-and-so on the president's staff
made a call to somebody else, to try to get them to, whatever
. . . 'I thought that's why you ran for president. I thought
that's why you became president, so you could affect the
actions that government took.'"[4]

Jane Pauley of NBC picked up the line, saying: "I read an
item in a magazine about Benjamin Franklin, saying that, as
he grew older, he learned he had the ability to change his
mind. Information, age, experience. We in the media don't
allow politicians to change their mind. We call that flip-flopping, or expedience."

Then Cokie Roberts of ABC said: "That is a really good
point, Jane, and it's one of the things that we've been talking
about a lot in this town lately. That if somebody makes com-
promises in order to get something done, that's considered
evil by us in the media—instead of saying that's what the
system requires. That's how you do govern: flip-flopping. We
have this notion that compromise is evil, or that learning and
maturing is something we should denigrate."

That, it seems to me, brings this little book back to its
beginnings. In denigrating politicians before the fact, before
we have reason, we are denigrating our own mission—and,
inevitably, ourselves. The mission is vigilance and understanding. Part of the mission is to understand where our
power ends. We have failed lately at trying to run the country. There are good things we can and should do—and there
are tasks we cannot do well because they are beyond our
reach or beyond public acceptability. There is courage and
honor in standing against the wind of calculated public opinion and checking out the emperor's wardrobe. But wisdom is

knowing when to shout and when to study, and understanding the difference between what we can do and what we should do.

We cannot stop the march of technology. It is a force of nature, as it was at the turning of the twentieth century, when development of the telegraph was followed by photography, the coast-to-coast railroad, telephones, rotary presses, electric light, moving pictures, automobiles, airplanes, and radio. Technology rules. A long time ago, the British press tried to control the role and growth of the British Broadcasting Corporation. The BBC, at first, was not allowed to gather news. All that BBC announcers were allowed to do on the air was read newspaper headlines after the papers had already appeared on the streets of London. That particular travesty lasted less than a year. Technology marches. I have served as a Pulitzer Prize juror, and the biggest press story of 1996 won neither prize nor mention. The story was that, for the first time, there were entries from the Internet. There were thirteen of them. We locked them away in a safe—to wait till next year.

We cannot do much about our owners—except to Yell All About It! in public if they are cheating the citizens, the voters, the readers, the viewers, the customers. When I started out as a reporter, advertising accounted for 50 percent of newspaper revenues. Now the proportion has passed 75 percent, which could be interpreted to mean advertisers are now at least three times as important as readers. In television, where viewing is free, advertisers are even more important. The networks defined their real role to be creating an audience for advertisers. Now that audience, and what advertisers want from the crowds, rule the creators. The free market, in both commerce and speech, means that just about everything goes to high bidders. Bigger and richer corporations rule or ruin smaller ones. Heads up: the new technological companies are more than ten times the size of the biggest media companies. Intel has 41,000 employees and annual revenues of more than $16 billion. Bell Atlantic: 62,000 employees and $13 billion. The New York Times companies and the Washington Post Company have a combined total of only 19,000 employees and combined revenues of about $4 billion.

What we *can* do something about is truth telling. That is where we, our rowdy tribe, has to fight or die—or both. "Media" is a combination of fact and fiction. Embellished fact and fabrication is the heart of the most powerful entertainments, from Greek drama to Shakespeare to *Uncle Tom's Cabin* to *Gone with the Wind* and the titillation tabloids. "Based on a true story" but "any resemblance to actual people living or dead is purely coincidental." Right! My family happened to be in Scotland the summer before the 1997 devolution referendum gave the Scots their first parliament in hundreds of years. To an American visitor, the single most important force behind the new wave of Scottish nationalism seemed to be an American semi-true historical epic. The film was *Braveheart,* in which Mel Gibson led dispossessed Scots against the cunning English. Closer to home, a film called *Hoodlum* showed New York district attorney Thomas E. Dewey shaking down mobsters—an obscene perversion of fact.

The issue is truth, not packaging. Hollywood, the world capital of entertainment, profits by adapting and inevitably distorting the news of the day into plausible fiction. Entertainment is a delicious lie, sometimes poisoned. But the sweetness of it may have something to do with a nation high on myths, more and more comfortable with or tolerant of deceit and lying.

Politicians quietly or casually lie, the honest ones doing it only when they have to. The military lies as a matter of course, seeing itself under siege by naïve outsiders, distrusting the press to the point of considering reporters the enemy and projecting only its own film and statements as news. War these days is brought home not by CNN but by PNN, the Pentagon News Network. During the Gulf War, an Associated Press reporter checked U.S. Army announcements of the capture of a small Kuwaiti town by telephoning the town hall and found himself speaking with an Iraqi lieutenant; then the reporter was attacked by the U.S. military as some sort of subversive. The White House lies: witness the false evidence and doctored tapes produced by the United States and provided to the United Nations during the debate in the case of KAL Flight 007, the Korean airliner shot down by the Soviet military over the Sea of Japan in 1983. The press lies, particularly in not being willing to admit that we rarely get the whole truth the first time around. To quote the president about us: "Perhaps an editor might divide his paper into four chapters: First, Truths; 2d, Probabilities; 3d, Possibilities; 4th, Lies."

That was President Thomas Jefferson, not William Jefferson Clinton.

We should stick close to the first chapter, the bottom line of real journalism. Probabilities, Possibilities, and Lies could be a working definition of entertainment. Being persistent and consistent, we should be a little obnoxious in exposing again and again what is provably not true and real. Be common scolds. Be annoying and self-righteous. Almost a century ago, Joseph Pulitzer grumbled: "A newspaper should be proud of the enemies it makes."

It's a dirty job, but somebody has to do it. We should not kid ourselves by thinking that other people and institutions cannot gather and distribute crucial information. They can, they are, and they will. We are being backed into a corner now by forces beyond our control—but most forces, like wind, change direction and ultimately die down. To survive and serve, we have to make our corner the one to which men and women of good will can repair, can come to find or verify truth and accuracy in a society under data siege.

I would prefer a Bill Brennan solution. Mr. Brennan, a citizen of the Borough of Queens, for a long time manned a telephone at the *New York Daily News*. It was the number you called to settle bets, to get the facts. Usually late at night, from a bar. With friends shouting in the background, you could call and ask questions like: What was Cookie Lavagetto's real name? Did Napoleon really say that a hostile newspaper is more to be feared than a thousand bayonets? Did Goethe really say, "What have the Germans gained by their boasted freedom of the press except the liberty to abuse one another"? Bill Brennan, walls of reference books around him, would settle the argument. (Harry Arthur Lavagetto. Yes, Napoleon and Goethe did say those things about us.) People would pay for that—for sure signposts in the information swamp. What is the real, not the mock? Where does nonfiction end and fiction begin? The truth may or may not make us free. But it will keep us working.

Could there be a better job than this commission from the people to safeguard their rights from the rich and powerful? I've never seen one. Humility and the determination to get it right are the only appropriate responses to such trust. I'm as romantic as good old Will Irwin, who thought publishers were just middlemen, downstairs selling tickets to the love affair between reporters and readers. Publishers, those old ignoramuses? No. No. Said Irwin, speaking of troubled times: "In the profession itself lies our greatest hope."

He saw reporters as a breed apart, as a class unto themselves. In other words, tribal—and outsiders. I'd like to believe that. In fact, I do believe it. There is a wild and charming naïveté among reporters that translates into both crankiness and a certain innocence about their own work and lives, particularly their relationship with the owners who inherited or hired them.

We are a tribe of romantic legends. This is one, told to me by Louis Boccardi, a New York reporter who became the president of the Associated Press:

In 1951, in Prague, Czechoslovakian police arrested the resident AP bureau chief, William Oatis, on charges of spying. At a communist show trial, the state prosecutor said: "This reporter is particularly dangerous because of his insistence on obtaining only accurate, correct, and verified information."

Oatis was convicted and spent two years in a Czech jail. Machines come and go. So do owners. But reporters endure and folks remember us for a few days. Perhaps our Humpty-Dumpty rise and fall during the past couple of decades will teach us something. We are best as outsiders, trying to function as an early-warning system, given the privilege of reporting back to a free nation. We do not have to be loved to do the job. In fact, we are most effective when we are insecure, doubting our inflated importance and self-importance and anyone's ability to catch truth and history on the fly. We deserve to be and should be outsiders looking in—that's all we are.

At the Republican National Convention in Miami Beach in 1972, I was squeezed into a hotel elevator with a group of ladies belonging to that Grand Old Party. They looked a lot like my mother and her friends.

"I smell something," one said.

"Reporter," said another, glancing toward me.

That was fair. They knew who they were, and I knew who I was. Each of us had a job to do. Mine was more fun, but they were right to distrust me. I was not one of them and never will be—I'm just a reporter.

. . . .

Notes · Acknowledgments · Index

Notes

Introduction

1. Jon Katz, www.hotwired.com, December 1997.
2. A. J. Liebling, *The Press* (New York: Ballantine, 1961), p. 3.
3. Herbert Gans, Author interview, 1997.
4. J. Randolph Murray, Address to the American Society of Newspaper Editors, Dallas, Texas, 1996.
5. Eli M. Noam, "Electronics and the Dim Future of Academic Publishers," unpublished paper, October 16, 1997, p. 2.

1. Covering the Naked Emperor

1. Thomas Babington Macaulay, quoted in William Safire, *Safire's New Political Dictionary* (New York: Random House, 1993), p. 264.
2. William Keller, Address at the Columbia University Graduate School of Journalism, December 4, 1997.
3. Stanley Walker, *City Editor* (New York: Harper's, 1932), p. 1.
4. Joseph Pulitzer, quoted in *North America Review* (New York), May 1904.
5. Wes Gallagher, quoted in Loren Ghiglione, *The American Journalist* (Washington, D .C.: Library of Congress, 1990), p. 81.

6. I. F. Stone, Author interview, July 1975.

7. Barney Frank, Author interview, December 4, 1997.

8. Potter Stewart, "Or of the Press," *Hastings Law Journal,* January 26, 1975, p. 633.

9. Oscar Wilde, *The Soul of Man under Socialism* (Boston: J. W. Luce, 1918), p. 58.

10. Ruth Marcus, "The White House Isn't Telling Us the Truth," *Washington Post,* August 21, 1994.

11. Elaine Sciolino, "Top U.S. Officials Divided in Debate on Invading Haiti," *New York Times,* August 4, 1994.

12. "The Rwanda Cable," *International Herald Tribune,* April 4, 1998, p. 10.

13. McGeorge Bundy to John F. Kennedy, May 16, 1961. National Security Files, Box 287-90, JFK Library, Boston.

2. Technology Happens

1. Robert L. O'Connell, "Post Haste," *American Heritage,* September–October 1989.

2. David Burke, Author interview, January 5, 1998.

3. Jon Katz, "Rock, Rap and Movies Bring You the News," *Rolling Stone,* March 5, 1992.

4. Edward Mack, *Peter Cooper, Citizen of New York* (New York: Mack Duell, Sloan and Pearce, 1949), p. 113.

5. Will Irwin, profile of James Gordon Bennett in *Collier's,* February 4, 1911, p. 15.

6. Jeremy Iggers, "Get Me Rewrite!" *Utne Reader,* September–October 1997.

7. Bill Gates, quoted in Mark Fitzgerald, "Fear Me Not," *Editor and Publisher,* May 3, 1997, p. 11.

8. Neil Hickey, "Will Gates Crush Newspapers?" *Columbia Journalism Review,* May 1997, p. 28.

3. If You Can't Beat 'Em, Buy 'Em

1. Richard Cohen, Author interview, November 15, 1997.
2. "Hate the News? Buy the Paper," *Editor and Publisher,* November 11, 1997.
3. Harry Evans, quoted in Doug Underwood, *When MBAs Rule the Newsroom: How the Marketers and Managers Are Reshaping Today's Media* (New York: Columbia University Press, 1993), p. 14.
4. W. H. H. Murray, in *The Arena,* October 1890, p. 553.
5. Will Irwin, in *Collier's,* April 22, 1911, p. 18.
6. Robert V. Hudson, *The Writing Game: A Biography of Will Irwin* (Ames: Iowa State University Press, 1982), p. 69.
7. George Seldes, *Freedom of the Press* (Indianapolis: Bobbs-Merrill, 1935).
8. Mark Willes, quoted in "National Journal Sale Was a Capital Secret," *Media Industry Newsletter,* June 16, 1997. Margaret T. Gordon, in *Media Studies Journal,* Summer 1995, p. 149. Robert Neuwirth, "Company Records Fall as Newspaper Profits Rise," *Editor and Publisher,* March 7, 1988, p. 22.
9. Mark Willes, quoted in "National Journal Sale Was a Capital Secret," *Media Industry Newsletter,* June 16, 1997.
10. Tom White, quoted in Jim Rosenberg, "Longtime Editor Quits in Lincoln," *Editor and Publisher,* April 26, 1997, p. 16.
11. David Burgin, quoted in Underwood, *When MBAs Rule the Newsroom,* p. 12.
12. Alison Carper, "Paint-by-Numbers Journalism," Discussion paper D-19, Shorenstein Center for Press, Politics, and Public Policy, Harvard University, April 1995, p. 18.
13. Gene Roberts, "Corporatism versus Journalism: Is It Twilight for Press Responsibility?" Press-Enterprise Lecture Series, no. 31, delivered at the University of California, Riverside, February 12, 1996.

14. Robert H. Giles and Jack Cox, "Are Journalists Too Ignorant to Cover Important News Issues Correctly?" *Editor and Publisher,* April 19, 1997, p. 11.
15. Gabe Pressman, "A Cop-Out?" *Columbia Journalism Review,* November–December 1997, p. 9.
16. Ted Koppel, Address before the Committee to Protect Journalists, New York City, October 23, 1997.

4. "The Tribe"

1. Lincoln Steffens, in *Collier's,* March 18, 1911, p. 20.
2. Marion Rodgers, ed., *The Impossible H. L. Mencken: A Selection of His Best Newspaper Stories* (New York: Anchor Books, 1991), p. 2.
3. Silas Bent, *Ballyhoo: The Voice of the Press* (New York: H. Liveright, 1927), p. 13.
4. Pete Hamill, "Newspapers for Working People," *Media Studies Journal,* Spring 1997, p. 87.
5. Bent, *Ballyhoo,* p. 55.
6. Will Irwin, *Collier's,* February 4, 1911, cover article.
7. Michael Bloomberg, Author interview, August 24, 1997.
8. Paul Voakes, *The Newspaper Journalist of the 1990s* (Washington, D.C.: American Society of Newspaper Editors, 1997).
9. "Profile of the News Consumer," *Editor and Publisher,* January 18, 1997.
10. Robert V. Hudson, *The Writing Game: A Biography of Will Irwin* (Ames: Iowa State University Press, 1982), p. 48.
11. David Gergen, Author interview, August 28, 1994.
12. James Ledbetter, "Bad News: The Slow, Sad Sellout of Journalism School," *Rolling Stone,* October 16, 1997, p. 74.
13. Ibid.

14. Lana Rakow, quoted in Betty Medsger, *Winds of Change: Challenges Confronting Journalism Education* (Arlington, Va.: Freedom Forum, 1996), p. 6.
15. *Larry King Live*, transcript, CNN, Washington, D.C., May 3, 1995.
16. William E. Simon, *A Time for Truth* (New York: McGraw Hill, 1978), p. 223.

5. "Give Them What They Want!"

1. Carl Ackerman, quoted in *Proceedings of the American Society of Newspaper Editors* (Washington, D.C.: ASNE, 1934), p. 54.
2. Wayne Ezell, quoted in Howard Kurtz, *Media Circus: The Trouble with America's Newspapers* (New York: Times Books, 1993), p. 348.
3. Doug Underwood, *When MBAs Rule the Newsroom: How the Marketers and Managers are Reshaping Today's Media* (New York: Columbia University Press, 1993), p. 181.
4. The following numbers are from *Changing Definitions of News: A Look at the Mainstream Press over Twenty Years,* released by the Project for Excellence in Journalism, March 4, 1998.
5. Eleanor Clift, quoted in *Newsday,* June 16, 1997, p. A21.
6. Albert Einstein, quoted in Leo Bogart, *Polls and the Awareness of Public Opinion* (New Brunswick, N.J.: Transaction Books, 1988), p. 47.
7. Bill Clinton, quoted in Richard Reeves, *Running in Place: How Bill Clinton Disappointed America* (Kansas City: Andrews and McMeel, 1996), p. 30.
8. Tony Blair, quoted in *The Scotsman* (Glasgow), August 20, 1996.
9. Newt Gingrich, quoted in the *New York Times,* October 27, 1995, p. 1.

10. Dan Rather, speaking on *Larry King Live,* transcript, CNN, Washington, D.C., March 28, 1995.
11. Stephen Koepp and Tom Hannon, quoted in news release, Time Inc., February 24, 1996.
12. Harry Smith, speaking on CBS News, transcript, May 27, 1993.
13. Sandy Berger, Author interview, October 1994.
14. Peter Hart, Author interview, August 24, 1997.
15. David Komansky, Author interview, July 8, 1997.
16. Av Westin, Author interview, October 12, 1997.

6. News as Entertainment

1. Ed Fouhy, Author interview, December 10, 1997.
2. Jane Pauley, speaking on *Larry King Live,* transcript, CNN, Washington, D.C., March 28, 1995.
3. J. Randolph Murray, quoted in Stanley E. Flink, *Sentinel under Siege: The Triumphs and Troubles of America's Free Press* (New York: Harper-Collins, 1997), p. 170.
4. Jerry Della Femina, Author interview, August 30, 1997.
5. Jane Pauley, speaking on *Larry King Live,* transcript, March 28, 1997.
6. Charles Lindbergh, quoted in George Seldes, *Freedom of the Press* (Indianapolis: Bobbs-Merrill, 1935), p. 263.
7. Sinclair Lewis, quoted ibid., p. 256.
8. Mark Crispin Miller, "Free the Media," *The Nation,* June 3, 1996.
9. Don Hewitt, quoted in the *New York Times,* August 15, 1997.

7. What's the Story?

1. James D. Squires, "Death of the Fourth Estate," *New Perspectives Quarterly,* Fall 1992.

2. Patrick Henry, quoted in William L. Rivers, *The Opinionmakers* (New York: Harper Colophon, 1975), p. 1.

3. Will Irwin, *Collier's*, April 1, 1911, p. 19.

4. Ann Richards, speaking on *Larry King Live*, transcript, CNN, Washington, D.C., May 3, 1995.

Acknowledgments

This book is based on the fifth Joanna Jackson Goldman Memorial Lecture, which I delivered at the Library of Congress on April 10, 1997. The Goldman Lectures, a series of talks on American institutions, were endowed by the historian Eric Goldman in memory of his wife. I was honored to be chosen and I am grateful for that to Daniel J. Kevles, representing the Goldman estate, and to Aida Donald of Harvard University Press. I am also indebted to James H. Billington, the Librarian, and two members of his staff: Prosser Gifford, director of the Office of Scholarly Programs, and Les Vogel.

I am, as always, in loving debt to my wife, Catherine O'Neill. President John F. Kennedy once said something like this of his brother Robert: "Bobby is the best man I have. With him around, all I have to do is show up." That's the way it is in our house. I'm the one who just shows up.

I chose to discuss the institution I know best, the American press. Writing about how I have made my living for more than thirty years was more fun than it should have been, considering that the subject is important and the institution itself seems to be in perpetual crisis—or perhaps it is just that the people who call themselves journalists perpetually worry and complain. But I became more optimistic about the future of the news business as I did research on new media and dredged up old memories.

The view was better than I expected partly because I did most of the writing high above Madison Avenue while on a fellowship provided by the Media Studies Center of the Freedom Forum, founded as the Gannett Foundation in mid-century by Frank Gannett, the father of the media chain that bears his name. I learned a good deal there from my fellow Fellows, a compatible bunch: Mike Godwin, Ying Chan, John Carey, Ken Dautrich, Sasha Torres, and Monroe Price. Scott Sherman, my research assistant there, guided me through libraries of journalism lore new to me. I owe special thanks to Lawrence McGill and Robert Giles of the Center, and to a long-time colleague and friend, Nancy Hicks Maynard, who introduced me to them.

Finally, I would like to mention two books I found particularly valuable: *Killing the Messenger—100 Years of Media Criticism*, edited by Tom Goldstein (Columbia University Press, 1989); and *Sentinel under Siege*, by Stanley E. Flink (Westview Press, 1997).

Index

ABC, 47, 102
ABC News, 30, 61, 65, 80–81, 85,
   90, 99, 101–102, 110–111, 124
Ackerman, Carl, 87–88
Alien and Sedition Laws (1798), 57
Al Smith Dinner, 77
American Newspaper Publishers
   Association, 51–52, 106
American Society of Newspaper
   Editors, 29, 32, 45, 87
America Online, 32, 44
Animal House, 108
Annenberg School for Communi-
   cation, 89
Anniston Star, 5, 104
Arena, The, 49
Associated Press, 12, 117, 127, 129
Atlanta Journal-Constitution, 9, 59

Baker, James, 23
Baltimore Sun, 49, 69
Begala, Paul, 76
Bell Atlantic, 126
Bellows, Jim, 59, 101
Bennett, James Gordon, 37–38, 67

Bent, Silas: *Ballyhoo,* 69–70
Berger, Samuel, 77, 95
Bernstein, Carl, 13, 78
Biagi, Shirley, 15
Blair, Tony, 92
Blake, Tiffany, 72
Bloom, Allan, 84
Bloomberg, Michael, 72–73, 114
Bloomberg Business News, 72, 114
Boca Raton News, 88
Boccardi, Louis, 129
Boggs, Hale, 85
Boggs, Lindy, 85
Boston Globe, 116
Bradlee, Ben, 59, 122
Brady Bill, 43
Braveheart, 126
Braver, Rita, 81
Brennan, Bill, 128
Breslin, Jimmy, 1
British Broadcasting Corporation,
   125
Broadcast News Network, 42
Brokaw, Tom, 88, 121–122
Bryan, William Jennings, 22

Buchanan, Pat, 85
Buchwald, Art, 75
Buckley, William F., 84
Bundy, McGeorge, 23
Bunyan, John: *The Pilgrim's Progress,* 15
Burgin, David, 59
Burke, David, 30
Bush, George, 23, 26

Cable News Network. *See* CNN
California gold rush, 26
Campbell, Julia, 63
Capital Gang, The, 76
Carroll, Maurice C., 1, 68
Carville, James, 76
CBS, 47, 55
CBS News, 24, 30, 41–42, 55, 63, 77, 81, 94, 110–111
Central Intelligence Agency, 26–27
Chandler family, 55
Changing Definitions of News, 89
Charlie Rose Show, 61
Chicago Tribune, 52, 59, 114–115
Civil War, 27, 107
Clift, Eleanor, 90
Clinton, Bill, 17–21, 25–27, 42, 75–76, 81, 83, 91–92, 94–95, 103, 116, 120
Clinton, Hillary Rodham, 19–20
CNN, 26, 70, 76, 81, 85, 94, 110, 123, 127
Coffee, Shelby, III, 59
Cohen, Richard, 47, 65
Collier's, 37, 50–53, 70–71, 113
Columbia University, 12, 78, 80
Committee to Protect Journalists, 65, 90

Congress, U.S., 16, 19, 57, 62, 92–93
Connable, Joel, 103
Constitution, U.S., 12, 16–17, 56
Contract with America, 93
Cosby, Bill, 103
Couric, Katie, 75
Cronkite, Walter, 104
Crosby, Steve, 60
Crossfire, 85
C-Span, 23
Cuomo, Mario, 77
Czechoslovakia, 129

Dallas Morning News, 121
Dallas Times Herald, 34
Dana, Charles A., 51
Dangerfield, Rodney, 83
Daniel, Clifton, 54
Dartmouth Review, 84
Dateline, 81, 102, 108
"Deep Throat," 22, 56
Defense Department, U.S., 22–24
Della Femina, Jerry, 106
Dempsey-Tunney fight, 69
Detroit Free Press, 45
Diana, Princess of Wales, 90–91, 103
Diogenes, 18, 115
Disney Company, 47, 64, 102, 110–111
Drudge, Matt, 120–121
Durk, David, 64

Editor and Publisher, 44, 54
Eisner, Michael, 47, 65
Elmira *Gazette,* 113
Entertainment Tonight, 99, 101–102
Evans, Harry, 49

Excite, 101
Express, 8
Ezell, Wayne, 88

Filo, David, 46, 48
First Amendment, 12, 16–17, 56
Forbes, 49, 96–98
Forbes, Steve, 63
Forrest Gump, 106
Fortune, 39
Fouhy, Ed, 101, 104
Fourth Estate, 8, 16–17, 118
Fox, 47
Fox News, 110
France, 118
Frank, Barney, 15
Franklin, Benjamin, 124
Freedom Forum, 113
Freeman, George, 64
Friedman, Thomas, 77–78
Fukuyama, Francis, 98

Gallagher, Wes, 12
Gallup Poll, 96
Gannett, Frank, 113
Gannett chain, 48, 113
Gans, Herbert, 5
Gates, Bill, 45
General Agreement on Tariffs and
  Trade, 76
General Electric, 47–48, 110–111
General Mills, 54–56
Gergen, David, 26, 75, 85
Gingrich, Newt, 93
Globe, 52
Goddard, Jacqueline, 46
Goethe, Johann Wolfgang von, 128
Gore, Albert, 25, 42–43
Greenfield, Jeff, 85

Grove, Andy, 29, 32–33, 45, 74
Gulf War, 26, 107, 127
Gutenberg, Johannes, 37

Haile, John, 29, 44
Haiti, 20, 25
Halberstam, David, 13
Hall, Arsenio, 18
Hamill, Pete, 69–70
Hannon, Tom, 94
Hard Copy, 99
Harding, Tonya, 117
Harper's, 33
Harris Poll, 96
Hart, Peter, 95–96
Hartford Courant, 49
Harvard Crimson, 67
Harvard University, 12
Hazlett, Thomas, 23
Hearst, William Randolph, 50
Hecht, Ben: *The Front Page,* 79
Henry, Patrick, 21, 118
Hewitt, Don, 110–111
Hewlett-Packard, 34–35
Heyward, Andrew, 77
Hoodlum, 126
Houston Post, 59
Hudson, Robert V., 74
Hunt, Al, 76

IBM, 31
Ingersoll-Rand, 2
Ingle, Bob, 45
Inside Edition, 101
Intel, 29, 45, 70, 126
International Herald Tribune, 64,
  134
Internet, 2, 32, 40, 44, 46, 70, 101,
  116, 120, 122, 125

Iraq, 26, 127
Irwin, Will, 15, 37, 50–53, 70–72, 74, 113–114, 118–119, 123, 129
Isikoff, Michael, 120

Jefferson, Thomas, 127
Jennings, Peter, 121–122
John M. Olin Foundation, 84
Johnson, Tom, 26
Joshi, Vyomesh, 35

Katz, Jon, 3, 34, 68
Keller, William, 9, 72
Kelly, Michael, 23
Kempton, Murray, 53–54
Kennedy, John, 23, 36, 39
Kerrigan, Nancy, 117
King, Larry, 18, 27, 81, 123
Kinsley, Michael, 75
Knight-Ridder chain, 45, 53
Koepp, Stephen, 94
Komansky, David, 97–98
Koppel, Ted, 65–66, 90–91
Korean Airlines flight 007, 127
Kovach, Bill, 59, 115, 122
Krauthammer, Charles, 81
Kristol, Irving, 84

Lake, Anthony, 20–22, 24–25, 76–77
Lamb, Brian, 23–24
Landay, Jerry, 41
Landsberg, Alan, 104
Lapham, Lewis, 33
Lear, Norman, 97
Lee Enterprises, 59
Lee Kuan Yew, 64
Leonsis, Ted, 32
Letterman, David, 87

Lewis, Sinclair, 110
Liebling, A. J., 4, 80
Limbaugh, Rush, 27, 83
Lincoln, Abraham, 27, 107
Lincoln Star Journal, 59, 115
Lindbergh, Charles A., 53
Lindbergh, Charles A., Jr., 53, 109–110
Lindsay, John, 1, 6
Live Video Insertion System, 34
Livingstone, David, 38
Los Angeles Times, 48–49, 55–56, 59, 73, 89, 115
Lott, Trent, 76
Lucent, 31

MacArthur, Charles: The Front Page, 79
Macaulay, Thomas Babington, 8
MacPherson, Sean, 33
Malone, John, 47
Marcus, Ruth, 18
Martin, Ron, 9
Masters, Edgar Lee: Spoon River Anthology, 58
McClure's, 37
McLaughlin, John, 85
McLaughlin Group, The, 90
McLuhan, Marshall, 102; Understanding Media, 33
McNamara, Robert, 24
Medicare, 93
Medill News Service, 89
Medsger, Betty: Winds of Change, 113
Meet the Press, 76–77
Megan's Law, 43
Mencken, H. L., 69
Meriwether, Heath, 45

Microsoft, 30–31, 34, 44–45
Miller, Susan, 88–89
Minneapolis Star-Tribune, 44
Molinari, Susan, 77
Morgensen, Gretchen, 63
Morrow, Anne, 109
Movie News, 102
Moynihan, Daniel Patrick, 76–77
MTV, 41
Muckrakers, 15–16, 118
Murdoch, Rupert, 47, 49, 110
Murray, J. Randolph, 5, 104
Murray, W. H. H., 49–50

Napoleon Bonaparte, 128
Nashville Tennessean, 42
National Enquirer, 24, 27, 36, 52
National Football League, 103, 105
National Security Council, 22
Naughton, James, 59, 115
NBC, 106, 108
NBC News, 26, 42, 77, 81, 88, 104, 108, 110–111, 124
NBC Sports, 105
Newark Evening News, 1–2
New Republic, 116
Newsday, 49
Newspaper Association of America, 45
Newsweek, 89–90, 120–121
New York Daily News, 69, 128
New Yorker, 4, 42, 80, 89
New York Herald, 37
New York Herald Tribune, 1, 10, 68, 101
New York Journal, 50
New York Post, 53–54, 72
New York Sun, 50–51, 71

New York Times, 1, 9, 20–21, 24, 27, 32, 34, 36, 42, 52, 54, 62–64, 67, 69–70, 72, 75–77, 85, 89, 93, 97
New York Times Company, 54, 126
Nicaragua, 107
Nielsen ratings, 97
Nightline, 61, 65, 90
Nixon, Richard, 11, 23, 76, 85
Nixon (film), 14
Noam, Eli, 5–6
Noonan, Peggy, 84

Oatis, William, 129
Olympics, 105
Orlando Sentinel, 29, 44
O'Rourke, P. J., 83

Pauley, Jane, 75, 81–82, 104, 108, 124
Pavlou, Tina, 41
PBS, 61
Pearl Harbor attack, 26
People, 90, 108
Perry, William J., 20
Peterson, Peter, 77–78
Pharmaceutical Manufacturers Association, 27
Philadelphia Inquirer, 59, 115
Phillipsburg Free Press, 2
Plimpton, George, 75
Polk, James, 26
Pony Express, 30
Pool, Ithiel de Sola, 57
Prigogine, Ilya, 42
Princeton Survey Research Associates, 61–62
Project for Excellence in Journalism, 61, 89

Prosser, Jeffrey, 47–48
Pulitzer, Joseph, 12, 80, 128
Pulitzer Prize, 125

Quayle, Dan, 81–82
Quindlen, Anna, 75

Rakow, Lana, 80
Rather, Dan, 81–82, 94, 121–123
Reagan, Ronald, 36
Reason, 23
Richards, Ann, 81–82, 123
Ridder, Herman, 52
Roberts, Cokie, 75, 81–82, 85, 124
Roberts, Eugene, 59
Robertson, Pat, 84
Roosevelt, Franklin, 26–27
Roosevelt, Theodore, 15–16
Rosenbaum, Steven, 41–42
Rosenthal, A. M., 54
R. R. Donnelley and Sons, 39
Russert, Tim, 75–77, 81–82, 85
Russo-Japanese War, 74

Safire, William, 83, 85
San Francisco earthquake, 71
San Francisco Examiner, 50
Sawyer, Diane, 75, 85
Schwarzkopf, Norman, 106–107
Sciolino, Elaine, 20, 25
Scotland, 126
Scripps chain, 52
Scripps-Howard, 88
Seldes, George, 109
Serpico, Frank, 64
Sharp Corporation, 40
Shawn, William, 88–89
Sherman, William T., 107
Shields, Mark, 85

Simon, William E.: *A Time for Truth,* 84
Simpson, O. J., 90–91, 117
Singapore, 64
60 Minutes, 111
Smith, Harry, 94
Smith, Susan, 117
Somalia, 27
Soviet Union, 98, 127
Squires, James, 59, 114–115
Stanley, Henry Morton, 38
Starr, Kenneth, 116
Steffens, Lincoln, 15, 67
Steinem, Gloria, 75
Stewart, Potter, 16–17
Stone, I. F., 14, 18
Stone, Oliver, 14
Sulzberger, Arthur, 54
Sulzberger, Arthur, Jr., 54

Talbott, Strobe, 20
Talese, Gay, 75; *The Kingdom and the Power,* 54
Tarbell, Ida, 15
TCI, 47
This Morning, 94
Time, 39, 63, 89–90, 94
Times (London), 49
Times/CBS Poll, 93
Times-Mirror Company, 48–49, 54–55
Time-Warner, 110
Tisch, Laurence, 55
Today, 26, 104
Travis, Neil, 72
Trollope, Anthony: *The Warden,* 58
Troutt, Kenny, 96–97
Turner, Ted, 98

Twain, Mark, 2
20/20, 99, 101–102

UNfiltered News, The, 41
University of California at Los Angeles, 78
University of Connecticut, 81
University of North Carolina Journalist, 60–61
University of North Dakota, 80
University of Southern California, 78, 89, 117
USAir Magazine, 75
U.S. Army, 127

Vietnam War, 11–14, 22–24
Virgin Islands Daily News, 47–48
Voice E-Mail, 31

Walker, Stanley, 10
Wall Street Journal, 40, 76, 83, 121
Washington Post, 13, 18, 25, 47, 64, 78, 122
Washington Post Company, 56, 126
Washington Star, 78
Watergate scandal, 11, 13–14, 23, 56, 122

Wausau Daily Herald, 60
Welch, Jack, 47
Westin, Av, 80, 99, 101, 108
Westinghouse, 47, 110–111
White, Tom, 59, 115
White House Radio and Television Correspondents Association, 17
Whitewater scandal, 18–19
Wilde, Oscar, 17
Will, George, 75, 83
Willes, Mark, 47–49, 54–56, 59
Williams, Jesse Lynch: The Stolen Story, 113–114
Wilson, Woodrow, 22
Windows '95, 30
Winfrey, Oprah, 18
Winston-Salem Journal, 60–61
Wolfe, Tom, 1
Woodward, Bob, 13, 56, 78; The Agenda, 75
World War I, 22, 69
World War II, 26–27, 92

Yahoo!, 44, 46
Yale Daily News, 67
Yang, Jerry, 46, 48, 116–117